The Works of Rev. David McGregor

1710-1777

William M. Gorman

HERITAGE BOOKS
2009

HERITAGE BOOKS
AN IMPRINT OF HERITAGE BOOKS, INC.

Books, CDs, and more—Worldwide

For our listing of thousands of titles see our website at
www.HeritageBooks.com

Published 2009 by
HERITAGE BOOKS, INC.
Publishing Division
100 Railroad Ave. #104
Westminster, Maryland 21157

Copyright © 2009 William M. Gorman

All rights reserved. No part of this book may be reproduced or transmitted in any form or by any means, electronic or mechanical, including photocopying, recording or by any information storage and retrieval system without written permission from the author, except for the inclusion of brief quotations in a review.

International Standard Book Numbers
Paperbound: 978-0-7884-4518-7
Clothbound: 978-0-7884-8168-0

The Works of Reverend David McGregor

CONTENTS

Preface
I

Introduction
III

Trial of the Spirits - 1741
1

Professors Warned of Their Danger – 1741
33

The True Believer's All Secured – 1747
59

The Christian Soldier – 1754
87

Address after the Right Hand of Fellowship - 1765
117

Christian Unity and Peace – 1765
120

An Israelite Indeed – 1774
142

The Voice of the Prophets Considered – 1776
165

Appendix
180

Preface

THESE are the works of my 6th great grandfather Reverend David McGregor also known as MacGregore or MacGregor, who's father brought his flock of Scotch-Irish immigrants to America in 1718 and settled in a part of New Hampshire called Nutfield which today is known as the towns of Derry and Londonderry.

This volume contains the known seven books of his sermons, the originals are very fragile today and since they have not been republished till now, I felt the originals would be best preserved by republishing his works. In this edition all his known sermons are included in one volume. The text and punctuation have been modified to modern American English standards for the ease of the reader. Script S's which look much like a lower case f, have been replaced with the modern s and I have for example changed some of the original "(1.) (2.) (3.)" with first, second and third, because it flowed much better and conformed to today's English. Some old expressions have been retained such as "&c." which is the equivalent of etcetera etcetera and the term "viz" which is an abbreviation for videlicer, which is used to introduce examples, lists, items or meaning "which is" or "as follows". Where possible viz has been replaced with the appropriate wording. In some instances where 'Tis was used, it was replaced with "It is". The last thing that is different in this edition is many words in the original were capitalized in the middle of sentences, which were not names or places and they have been changed to lower case letters.

The picture on the cover is a virtual portrait of David at his home it contains a picture of David's house as it would have appeared in 1740. No portrait of David McGregor is know to exist so I used a picture of my late father for a likeness.

Rev. David McGregor's sermons are very much ahead of his time and sheds light on the religious sentiments of colonial New

II   The Works of Reverend David McGregor

England. He questions the old scriptures and seems to have believed in experimenting in new beliefs and new forms of religion, which is very revolutionary for his time.

Three of the sermons were found in the town of Chester, Vermont, which was very near the residence of David McGregor's daughter and my 5th great grandmother Margaret McGregor-Rogers. Margaret had married Captain James Rogers, brother of the famous Major Robert Rogers of Rogers Rangers. For her husbands service in the French and Indian War James Rogers was granted sixty two square miles of Vermont which was know as the township of Kent and later in 1795 and 1797 split in two becoming the townships of Londonderry and Windham, Vermont. The nearest Church to their homestead was in neighboring township of Chester, which is where the people of Kent went for worship.

Trial of the Spirits is from 1741, not long after a sermon about the spirit by Reverend John Wesley and the controversy caused by letters from George Whitefield in August of 1740. From what I see in the sermon of Wesley and Whitefield's letter, it seems much of the dispute was a misunderstanding and a difference of opinion which Reverend McGregor takes neither side and suggests that the individual makes their own conclusion based on their own faith and beliefs.

Professors Warned of their Danger is directed at ministers of the gospel. It is a guide to the minister of their responsibilities and duties as a teacher of the gospel. It also warns them of the consequences of careless, insensitive and dangerous practices of their teachings.

The True Believer's All Secured seems to be aimed at assuring the people of God's promise to take care of the faithful.

The Christian Soldier is an ordination sermon and David covers the duties and troubles of being a minister.

Introduction

Reverend David McGregor
November 6, 1710 – May 30, 1777
Presbyterian Minister
of Londonderry, New Hampshire

David McGregor was born in Aghadowey, Londonderry, Ireland November 6, 1710, he was the first son of Rev. James McGregor. In 1718 his family along with his father's flock migrated to Massachusetts Bay Colony and was granted land in New Hampshire at a place called Nutfield. In May of 1719 Reverend James McGregor conducted the first Presbyterian service in New England, offering the installation prayer and preaching the installation sermon. His sermon was based on Ezekiel 37. 26. "Moreover I will make a covenant of peace with them; it shall be an everlasting covenant with them; and I will place them and multiply them, and will set my sanctuary in the midst of them for evermore."

On June 3rd 1720 at a public meeting it was voted that a small house be built "convenient for the inhabitants to meet in for the worship of God," and it should be placed "as near to the center of the one hundred and five lots as can be convenience."

Reverend James McGregor claimed "there is just three kinds of songs. There is the very good song, the very bad song, and the song that is neither bad nor good. 'While Shepherds Watch Their Flocks by Night' is a very good song, 'Janie Stoops Down to

IV   The Works of Reverend David McGregor

Buckle Her Shoe' is a very bad song. But 'Sue Loves Me and I Loves Sue' is neither good nor bad."

Introduction v

David McGregor's gravestone is inscribed as follows.

Memento mori
Etsi mors indies accelerat tamen
Virtus post Funera vivet
Here lies the dust of him who did proclaim
Salvation to lost souls in Jesus' Name
His Master dated to give the great reward
To those who here flock of Christ regard
The Rev Mr. David MacGregore Son of
The Rev. James MacGregore first
Minister in Londonderry
Deceased the 30th of May AD 1777
In the 68th year of his age
To his memory this monument
Is erected by his Relict and Children

Mrs. Mary MacGregore
Relect of
Rev. David McGregore
Died Sept 28, 1793
Aet 70

VI   The Works of Reverend David McGregor

Grave of David McGregor

Rev. David McGregor was buried in the Forest Hill Graveyard in East Derry, New Hampshire.

Introduction   VII

Rev. David McGregor married Mary Boyd a daughter of James Boyd in 1734 and he was ordained in 1737. They had eight children, David born about 1737, Margaret born about 1740 married Captain James Rogers of Rogers Rangers a brother of Major Robert Rogers, Mary born about 1744 married Mayflower descendant James Hopkins, James born about 1748 married Margaret Holland, Robert born about 1749 married Elizabeth Reid, Mary (2) born December 6, 1752 married Robert Means, Jane birth date unknown married Robert Hunter, Elizabeth birth date and marriage unknown.

One son of David McGregor's, Robert McGregor Esquire 1749 - 1816 built the first bridge over the Merrimack River in August and September of 1792. This bridge was known as McGregor's Bridge and crossed the river from near his home in Goffstown on the west side to what is today Bridge Street in Manchester, New Hampshire. Today McGregor Street parallels the River on the west side along the old Amoskeag Mill building.

Another son of David McGregor's, James McGregor 1748 – 1818 was a New Hampshire state senator representing Rockingham County for two years 1793 -1794.

David's father, James McGregor is thought to be a first cousin of the famous Robert Roy McGregor. David's grandfather was Colonel David McGregor who was born in Balquhidder, Perthshire, Scotland, the same location of Rob Roy McGregor's burial. James insisted he was Scottish and not Scotch-Irish.

David's father, Reverend James McGregor brought his family, along with three other pastors and their flocks on 5 ships to America, as James put it to "avoid opposition and cruel bondage, to shun persecution and designed ruin, to withdraw from the communion of idolators and to have an opportunity of worshipping God according to the dictates of conscience and the rules of his inspired word". James studied in Europe and graduated from the University of Glasgow was ordained in 1701. James lead the first Presbyterian service in New England under a tree by the lake in what is now East Derry, New Hampshire. His sermon on Ezekiel 37. 26: "Moreover I will make a covenant with them; it shall be an everlasting covenant with them; and I will place them and multiply them, and will set my sanctuary in the midst of them for evermore. On January 11, 1721 the town voted to erect a meeting house in the center of town and construction began the following summer. The town avoided Indian incursions because the French Governor of Canada Marquis de Vaudreuil was a collage classmate of Reverend McGregor's and instructed the native to not harm the people of Nutfield, that they were different and not like the English.

David McGregor was the first minister of the West Parish of Derry and until he died in 1777, forty families from the East Paris worshiped in the West Parish and visa-versa West to East. The residents chose to pay their worship tax to the adjacent town. Seems the problems with the different religious sects truly divided the town. The townspeople would cross paths on the way to worship. People were known to carry their shoes for miles until they got to the church.

First Lady, Mary Means Appleton-Pierce, wife to President Franklin Pierce was David McGregor's great granddaughter.

David McGregor was also in one instance known to have practiced law. Around 1750 a wealthy resident of Portsmouth named John Odiorne received two letters demanding 500 pounds to be left at the western end of the long bridge between Kingston and Chester. The letter threatened to burn Mr. Odiorne's property and kill his family if the demands were not met. After the money was placed a reputable citizen of Londonderry, Captain John Mitchell happened along and dismounted his horse nearby. Captain Mitchell was arrested by a guard stationed to watch the loot and charged with the crime. He had protested his innocence and was unable to obtain an attorney for his defense. Even though Captain Mitchell was not a member of Rev. David McGregor's church, David was convinced of Captain Mitchell's innocence and offered to represent him. Although Rev.

Introduction IX

McGregor had no knowledge of court proceedings, he managed to defend Captain Mitchell elegantly and presented a strong argument. The court however convicted Captain Mitchell and fined him one thousand pounds. Because he was unable to pay the fine he was placed in jail until Rev. McGregor paid a bail for his release. After some time new evidence was discovered which proved his innocence and Captain Mitchell was acquitted.

In the year 1751-52 Captain Charles Stinson commenced a settlement in Starkstown (afterward Dunbarton), where for a time he lived alone in a log cabin, in which, on one occasion, he received as a visitor the Rev. David McGregore. "Not having a table," says the historian of Londonderry, "nor anything that would answer as a better substitute, he was obliged to make use of a basket, turned up." The Rev. Mr. McGregore, in asking a blessing, pertinently implored that his host might be "blessed in his basket and in his store." This blessing was literally fulfilled, as Mr. Stinson became one of the wealthy persons in the vicinity.

David McGregor's original home located on the Douglas Wise Farm on Warner Hill Rd. in East Derry, New Hampshire was still standing in the Fall of 2005 when I took this photo. Upon revisiting the site on March 12th, 2006, sadly the current owner Mr. Wise being not so wise has demolished the home and all that remained was the cellar.

Mr. McGregere's SERMON
ON THE
Trial of the SPIRITS.

THE
Spirits of the present Day Tried.

A
SERMON
At the Tuesday Evening-Lecture in
Brattle-Street, BOSTON, Nov. 3, 1741.

By the Reverend
Mr. David McGregore,
Of Londonderry in New England.

With a PREFACE by some Ministers of Boston.

I. Thess. V. 21. Prove all Things: hold
fast that which is Good.

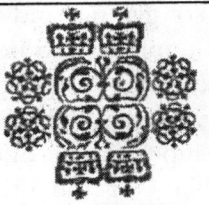

BOSTON, Printed by D. Fowle for D.
Henchman in Cornhill. 1742

The PREFACE.

AS all the Protestant Churches in Europe, both Episcopalian and Presbyterian most happily agreed at the time of the reformation in the scripture doctrines of grace, as appears by the harmony of their confessions published; in particular, the Church of Scotland in 1560, the Church of England in 1562, 3, and the Church of Ireland in 1616; so it must be own'd that the Presbyterians have generally persevered in a steady adherence to the original doctrines of the reformation, to the present day.

And as the assembly's shorter Catechism has been all along agreeable to the known principals of the New England Churches, and has been generally received and taught in them as a system of Christian doctrine agreeable to the Holy scriptures, wherein they happily unite; It is a great pleasure to us that our Presbyterian brethren who come from Ireland are generally with us in these important points, as also in the particular doctrines of experimental piety arising from them, and the wondrous works of God agreeable to them at this day making its triumphant progress through the land: all now happily combining to illustrate and confirm each other in so glaring and strong a manner as is irresistible to serious and unprejudiced beholders; and has already forced many men of clear minds, strong powers, considerable knowledge, and firmly riveted in the Arminian and Socinian tenets, to give them all up at once and yield to the adorable sovereignty and irresistibility of the divine spirit in his saving operations on the souls of men.

For to see on the one hand such men as these, some of them of licentious lives, long inured in a course of vices, and of high spirits, coming to the preaching of the word, some only out of curiosity, others with a strong antipathy and mere design to get matter of caviling and banter; all at once in opposition to their inward enmity, resolutions, and resistances, to fall under an unexpected and hated power; to have all the strength of their resolution and resistance taken away; to have such an inward view of the horrid wickedness not only of their lives, but also of their hearts, which their exceeding great and immediate danger of eternal misery, as has amazed their souls and thrown them into distress unutterable, yea forced them to cry out in the assemblies with the greatest agonies: and then in two or three days and sometimes sooner, to have such unexpected and raised views of the infinite grace and love of God in Christ, as have enabled them to believe in him, lifted them at once out of their distresses, filled their hearts with admiration and joy unspeakable and full of glory, breaking forth in their shining countenance and transporting voices to the surprise of those about them: And to see them kindling up at once into a flame of love and praise to God, an utter detestation of their former courses and vicious habits, yea by such a detestation the very power of those habits at once receive a mortal wound: in short to see their high Spirits on a sudden humbled, their hard hearts made tender, their aversion from the Holy God now turned into a powerful and prevailing bent to contemplate upon him as revealed in Christ, to labor to be like him in Holiness, to please and honor him by a universal and glad conformity to his will and nature, and to promote his holy Kingdom in all about them, abounding in acts of justice, charity, in a meek and condescending carriage towards the meanest, and aspiring after higher sanctity....

And to see other gentlemen of the knowledge, parts and principals, and of sober, just and religious lives, as far as their mere reason with outward revelation are able to carry them, and prepossessed against this work as imagined enthusiasm; yet at once surprisingly to find themselves entirely destitute of that inward Sanctity and supreme love to God and Holiness which the gospel teaches as absolutely needful to the Kingdom of grace and glory; to find themselves no more than conceited Pharisees, who had been working out a righteousness of their inward enmity to Christ and the nature and way of redemption by him, with the native vileness of their hearts and lives they had never seen before: In short to find themselves yet unrenewed in the spirit of their minds, and under the heavy wrath and curse of God; to open into clear discovery of their path delusions; to find the hardness of their hearts, the blindness of their minds, their utter impotence to convert themselves or believe in Christ; to loose all their former confidence, give up their beloved schemes, see themselves undone and helpless, and sink into great distress: and then condemning themselves as guilty wretches humbly lying at the foot of absolute and sovereign grace, and looking up to the glorious God, to justify them wholly by his own most perfect righteousness, and to enlighten, quicken, sanctify, dwell in and govern them by his almighty spirit; and their to wait till they find a new & mighty life & power come into their souls, enabling them to embrace, truth in and love this divine redeemer, rejoice with satisfaction in him, and perform every kind of duty both to God & man with pleasure and with quite another frame and spirit than before…

Such great and sudden turns as these are as evident demonstrations as we can possibly conceive of the truth of the inspired scriptures, and in particular of those scripture doctrines of the sovereign and victorious grace of Christ, received and taught among us. We see with our eyes, that when he rideth forth on the word of truth conquering and to conquer, his right hand teaches terrible things, he makes his arrows so sharp and precise in the hearts if his stoutest enemies, as oblige them to fall down under him; and when the day of his power comes on any people, He makes the most obstinate to be most gladly willing and obedient to him: And these principles of grace, and these works of God do most invincibly confirm each other.

And though it must be owned with sorrow that some few who see these wondrous works continue unconvinced; yet this is no more strange than that some of the most learned and religious men, as were the Scribes & Pharisees who saw the wondrous works of Christ on Earth, yet continued unconvinced that they were the works of God, yea pursued him with unrelenting enmity and violence. However, it is a reviving consolation to us, that as this work surprisingly goes on from town to town, it goes on more and more to silence the most fierce opposers: through mighty oppositions rife at first, it bares them down before it; and our more mighty savior seems resolved to go on still from conquering to conquer.

In vain do its remaining enemies attempt to brand it with the name—enthusiasm. For this is like the gentile Romans branding the Jewish Religion with the hated name of superstition; and if this work is truly enthusiasm, then we have been wholly mistaken in the meaning of the word: and what they call enthusiasm is a glorious and blessed work of God, most powerfully and suddenly changing the very hearts and lives of men; making them in a great degree like to Christ in love and righteousness and Holiness and meekness and humility; filling their hearts with holy joy and their mouths with praises.

But we must remit the remaining opposers to the law and testimony of God and dear brother the author of the following valuable sermon does. And we are glad on this occasion to join our testimony with him, both to the same doctrines of grace and to the wondrous works of God agreeable to them; as also to declare our great Satisfaction to see him and others of our said Presbyterian brethren concurring with us in them: with our apprehension that our uniting in these important Points, is such a powerful band of union in Christian love and fellowship as should overcome the remains of every kind of prejudice that may yet subsist among our people: and our earnest wishes that with a tender and meek forbearance of each other in different sentiments about church order and government, we may all unite in maintaining and promoting these more excellent and momentous points of grace and vital piety.

Boston, Jan. 12, 1741,2.	Thomas Price
	John Webb
	William Cooper

1 John IV. 1.

Beloved, believe not every Spirit, but try the Spirits whether they be of God: because many false Prophets are gone out into the World.

E read Rev. 12. 12. That the Devil came down among the inhabitants of the Earth having great wrath because he knew his time was short. When the strong man armed keepeth his place, all his goods are in peace: every thing is then as he would have it to be: his subjects go sleeping on to Hell, and imagine themselves all the while in the direct way to Heaven. But on the other hand, when he perceives that his policies begin to be detected, the eyes of his slaves to be opened to see their misery and their need of the remedy, and that by this means his Kingdom appears to be going to wreck; when he sees the standard of the great Messiahs erected and the gathering of the people about it; when he sees them flock thereto as a cloud and as the doves to their windows; that men are daily deserting his government by hundreds and thousands and going over to Christ the great deliverer. When (I say) he holds things having such an appearance, he then thinks it is high time for him to bestir himself, and if possible to support his tottering empire. To this end he

convocates the black Divan, takes counsel how he may mar God's work most effectually: and in pursuance of his counsel he finds it sometimes necessary to transform himself into an Angel of light, and to send forth his ministers; who thought inward they are ravening wolves, yet they come in sheep's clothing: and partly by hellish lies, partly by aggravating some real indiscretions, partly by false parallels, perverting some texts of scripture, and misapplying others; they put some of the weaker even of God's own children to a stand to that degree that they know not for some time what to say: so they would deceive (were it possible) the very elect.

Thus it is in this glorious day of gospel grace. As the good spirit appears to be striving in a remarkable manner; so Satan and his instruments, we have reason to think, are very industrious. Yea so cunningly does this insidious adversary manage, that he sometimes gets good men engaged upon his side. We have great reason to fear that it is now a time in various places in which there is ground for the repeating of God's complaint by his prophet Hos. 4. 6. My people are destroyed for lack of knowledge; that those who lead them cause them to error: and that by this means God's name continually every day is blasphemed. But blessed be God, that we have our bibles. So that if it should happen at any time that those whose lips out to preserve knowledge, should themselves turn aside from the ways of God either in doctrine or morals; that in this case we are not obliged to follow them implicitly, but that we have a sure World of prophesy even the law and testimony for our rule, and also the promise that if we ask the Holy Spirit we shall receive him. In sum, we have great reason to be thankful that our God has given us liberty and put us in a capacity of judging for our selves. That I may therefore have an opportunity of showing the necessity and importance of using this our Christian liberty aright in trying the spirits whether they be of God; I have chosen to speak from the above text as the ground of the following discourse: where the apostle says, beloved, believe not every spirit, but try the spirits whether they be of God: &c.

It may not perhaps be amiss to observe briefly, that the penman of this epistle was the evangelist and beloved disciple John: the particular time when he wrote it is uncertain: the persons to whom he wrote it are said to be Jews: not those that dwelt in Judea, but those who lived in the Eastern part of Asia, which is in the Empire of Parthia... The scope of the apostle in this epistle is, partly to prove, that Jesus of Nazareth is the true Messiahs; not only to induce men steadfastly to believe this great fundamental, but to impress the truth of it upon their souls in a more deep, lively and practical manner; partly to reduce the licentious, to raise the spiritually vigorous Christianity; and partly to excite Christians to the duty of mutual love, which seems to have been this beloved disciple's favorite subject.

More particularly in the words we have. First a caution, second a duty enjoyed, third a motive to the performance of said duty.

First a caution in these words, beloved, believe not every spirit. The term spirit is here by a figure put for the person who is acted by a spirit whether good or bad. It is q. d. believe not every person pretending to inspiration, or to be the messenger of God: don't be so credulous and implicit as to suffer your selves to be imposed upon by every one who says he has a commission from Heaven...

The second thing in the words, is a duty enjoyed in these words, try the spirits. q. d. Christ your gracious master has forbidden you to be the servants of men, or to pin your faith upon any man's sleeve. You are therefore to be followers of no man farther than he is of Christ nay your master has not only allowed you to judge for yourselves, but he has put you in a capacity so to do to this end he has made you reasonable creatures, and given you his word in your native language. Imitate the Bereans therefore, search the scriptures daily with all readiness of mind, to see if the things that are spoken be so.. But then the third thing in the words is a motive to the performance of the duty enjoyed in the words, because many false prophets are gone out into the world. q. d. You ought to be very careful in trying the spirits, inasmuch as these last times are perilous times, the world is full of deceivers: Take head therefore and beware of these false teachers. Remember that it is not all gold that glitters; that Satan himself is often transformed into an angel of light; that many pretend to come in God's name with a thus saith the Lord in their mouths, whom he has not sent, Fer. 29. 8, 9. Has not your master warned you that false Christs and false prophets shall arise, and shall show great signs and wonders, to deceive (were it possible) the very elect. You had great need then to be cautiously upon your guard.

The method I design in the prosecuting of this subject shall be to speak somewhat to each of these following heads.

I. First, I shall briefly show that there have always been false prophets or teachers in the World, who have pretended to Inspiration.

II. Secondly, that God has graciously been pleased to give his church a certain and invariable rule, by which they distinguish between the spirit of truth and the spirit of error.

III. Thirdly, that 'tis highly necessary, that Christians make good use of this rule, in trying the spirits and judging for themselves.

IV. Fourthly, I shall endeavor to try the spirits which have been the instrumental cause of that religious commotion in various parts of this continent and elsewhere, to see if they be of God ...

V. And lastly, I shall conclude with some brief application of the subject.

I. I begin with the first of these heads in order, which is to show that there have been always false prophets or teachers in the

World, who have pretended to inspiration or divine revelation. That this is a truth any person who is acquainted with sacred and profane history will readily grant. If we look into sacred history during the Old Testament period we shall find a multitude of the Devil's ministers, all pretending to divine inspiration, I might show a great many particular instances. We have God warning his people, Duet. 13. 12. of false teachers who should endeavor cunningly to draw them aside from the worship of the true God to that of idols. Thus we read 2 Tim. 3 8. that there was a James and a Jambres in the court of Pharaob who withstood Moses, and who by sorcery and the help of the Devil thought to do as a great miracles as Moses did by the infinite power of God. And thus Balaam, notwithstanding his high pretences to divine revelation and also to the most inflexible integrity; yet was one who dealt with the Devil in hellish spells and enchantments, and also a person of a base, mercenary, covetous disposition. And then if we come down to the days of Elisha, we find the prophets of Baall were very numerous, and also exceeding zealous in their way, in so much that they leaped upon the alter and cut themselves with knives and lancers till the blood gushed out. And thus we read that there was a Zedekiah to oppose Micaiah the true prophet of the Lord, and to persuade Abab to go to rameth Gilead to his own ruin. Thus there were lying prophets, in the days of Jeremiah, who persuaded Zedekiah and his people that Jerusalem should not fall into the hands of Chaldeans; and by this means led that poor unhappy prince and his people to their ruin, by hindering them to make that seasonable capitulation which might have prevented it.

And then if we turn our eye from the sacred history of the Old Testament to the profane histories that are co-incident with and after that period, we shall find innumerable cheats and imposters of this sort. He must need to be a stranger to or at least superficially acquainted with the Grecians, the Romans and other Pagan histories, who has not heard of the famous Sibylline Oracles, of the oracle of Apollo at Delphos, that of Diana at

Ephesus, as likewise that of Jupiter Hamon in Libya, with many others: the respective priests of which all pretended to be inspired by their Gods when they gave forth the oracular answers. Who has not heard of the two famous imposters which is. Zoroastres in Persia and Mahomet in Arabia.

And if we take a view of the New Testament period, and the time that has since ensued, we shall find that no sooner did the light of the gospel shine out and the glorious Sun of righteousness irradiate the World with his illuminating and cheering beams, but the prince of darkness endeavored to obscure it. Where there not those even in the days of the apostles who erred in the great doctrine of justification, who were for mixing the deeds of the law along with faith, and who taught that we are justified partly by faith and partly by works? Whose pernicious tenants the apostle Paul refutes in a solid and elaborate manner in his Epistles to the Romans and Galatians. Were there not those who quarreled with and impugned the high and sovereign doctrine of predestination, whose cavils the apostle answers in the ninth chapter to the Romans. Thus the apostle Peter tells us of unlearned and unstable men who wrested scriptures to their own destruction. Do we not read of ungodly men who turned the grace of our Lord Jesus Christ into lasciviousness; who under pretence of exalting free grace, unloosened the reins on the neck of their impetuous lusts saying, let us continue in sin that grace may abound? Were there not an Himeneus and Philetes, who denied the resurrection, and overthrow the faith? Was there not an Ebion who denied the divinity of Christ, and who taught the obligation of the ceremonial law under the gospel? A Cerinthus who taught that Christ should at his coming give to his people all carnal or sensual delights, and who denied the whole scripture, Mathew's gospel excepted. What vile principles did the Gnosticks hold? What abdominal practices were they guilty of? And yet what high pretences were they guilty of? And yet what high practices to revelation did they make?

If we come further down and look into the legends of the Church of Rome; how many ridiculous stories, how many counterfeit miracles, & lying wonders have we there? And then if we descend still further down and come to the time of reformation, we shall find that no sooner did that blessed day of gospel light break forth upon the World, but the Devil endeavored to obscure it. How many extravagant sects, how many heretical opinions showed themselves in the days of the reformers? The respective patrons of which all pretended to be zealous Protestants, and to make a loud cry against the Church of Rome? He who will be at pains to read the history of the German Anabaptist, the gross errors and ridiculous extravagancies they run into; as also that of some of the sectaries in South Britain in the last century; as likewise the rife and progress of the subtle error of Arminius; cannot but grant the point.

Thus from what has been briefly said this head, it plainly appears that there have been always false teachers in the World who have pretended to inspiration, as far as we have any history to inform us. And it is very probable it will be so as long as the Devil has a Kingdom in the World. But what I pray do the adversaries of the perfect religious commotion gain by the proving of this point, except they can likewise prove that the promoters of the present work hold the same pernicious principles, or as bad as those ancient heretics did; or that they are guilty of the same wicked practices that those were? Does it indeed follow as a just consequence that because Arius, Socinus, Pelagius, Arminius, &c. were heretics and false teachers; that therefore Messieurs the Erskines in Scotland and their adherents there, Dr. Edwards and Mr. Whitefield in the Church of England and their adherents there, are also heretics and false teachers; especially considering that they oppose those ancient heretics, and in opposition to them do maintain the doctrines of the 39 articles of the Church of England, and those of the Westminster concession of faith? He who can make a just consequence of this, may reconcile light and darkness, and prove that bitter & sweet are the same things.

II. I proceed to the second thing, which is to show that God has been graciously pleased to give his Church a complete and invariable rule, by which they may distinguish between the spirit of truth and the spirit of error. I need not dwell long on this head. It is only necessary to observe briefly, that the Holy scriptures contained in the several books of the Old Testament is this rule, I presume your all hold at least by profession; that the scripture is the word of God, and consequently the great rule of faith and practice. I shall not therefore at present stay upon the proof of that which is granted upon all hands. And he who grants this, that the scripture is only rule, will be obliged to admit of particular text taken out of scripture to prove that it is a complete rule. And of these are abundance: see Psal. 19. 8. The law of the Lord is perfect converting the soul, &c. Thus Mic. 6. 8. He hath showed thee, O man what is good, &c. To the same purpose is 2 Tim. 3. 16. All scripture is given by inspiration of God; and is profitable for doctrine, for reproof, for the man of God may be perfect, &c. And it is a mercy for which we cannot be too thankful, that we have this rule, and are not obliged to receive as doctrines the commandments of men. Who had they the leading of our judgments and consciences, would soon (we have reason to fear) bring us to burlesque all serious godliness, and to ridicule the operations of the blessed spirit under the notion of enthusiasm and delusions.

When I say the Scripture is a complete rule, and that God has thereby put his people into a capacity to distinguish between the spirit of truth and the spirit of error; I would by no means be understood to exclude the necessity of the spirit's teachings. Christ, as a prophet, teaches by his spirit, as well as by his word: yea and the teachings of the spirit is absolutely necessary in order to the saving and practical understanding of the word. A person indeed may possibly attain a sound and right doctrinal knowledge without the spirit, so as to approve of the things that are excellent, being instructed out of the law, Rom. 2. 18. and by this means may be so far judge of doctrine, as to try the spirits aright. But a saving practical knowledge he cannot attain without the teaching of the spirit: nor does this in any way derogate from the completeness and perfection of the rule: 'tis not owing to any defect in the Sun, that a blind eye cannot see the light.

III.   I pass to the third thing in the method; which is to show that 'tis highly necessary that Christians make good use of the rule that God has given them, in trying the spirits and judging for themselves.

That is a truth, is plain from the words of my text: Try the spirits, &c. To this purpose we have the injunction 1 Thess. 5. 21. Prove all things, hold fast that which is good. Thus Phil. 1. 9, 10. The apostle prays on the behalf of that Church, that their love may grow more and more in knowledge and in all judgment, that they may approve the things that are excellent. And thus Heb. 5. 13, 14. The apostle speaks of grown or experienced Christians, who he says have their senses exercised to discern both good and evil. The apostle desires the Corinthians to be followers of him no further than he was of Christ, 1 Cor. 11. 1. which plainly shows that they had a right to try him, and his doctrines, by the rule. Thus we have the bereams commended, and the epithet of noble given them, for their assiduous care in searching the scriptures to see if the things spoken even by the apostles were so. Acts. 17. 11. And it is spoken to the just praise of the Church of Ephesus, Rev. 2. 2. That she had tried those who said they were apostles, and had found them to be liars. Which agrees our Lord's injunction to the disciples, John 5. 39. Search the scriptures.

In the sum, God has graciously allowed Christians, as a part of their Christian liberty, a judgment of discretion: and this is their duty to hold fast, making good use of the powers that God has endowed them withal as reasonable creatures, in trying the spirits by the rule of God's word: bringing all private Spirits and all particular doctrines to this great infallible standard, this platform of faith and manners; as they agree or disagree with it, receiving or rejecting them. Isa. 8. 20. To the law and to the testimony; if they speak not according to this word, it is because there is no light in them.

IV. I come now to the fourth and last thing proposed in the doctrinal part, which was to try the spirits which have been the instrumental cause of that religious commotion in various parts of this continent and elsewhere, to see if they be of God. As this (in the present conjuncture) is the most material head, I shall endeavor to be somewhat larger upon it: And what I may proceed the more distinctly I shall essay to try first the spirit of the promoters, second of the opposers of the present work: and then let everyone judge for himself and say, which appears to be most of God. But ere I proceed I would beg leave to premise a few things:

1. I premise that it is very unjust to charge any party in general with the erroneous opinions or imprudent conduct of one or more particular persons who have declared themselves to be of the party. Especially if said party be so far from approving of or countenancing said opinions and conduct, that they declare against them, and take due care as far as circumstances will allow, to deal with the person or persons in order to his or their reformation. As for example, I appeal to the errors & ridiculous extravagances of the German Anababtists? Or the Church of England with those of Whiston? Would it have been just in a common enemy of Christianity to charge Paul with the dissimulation of Peter, when he withstood him to the face in that wherein he was to be blamed? And in the manner would it be just to charge Mr. Whitefield with the errors of Mr. Wesley? Thus in case any of the present work in the land should run into any errors, or he guilty of any extravagant conduct; would it be just to make this a matter of reproach to the whole work?

2.   I would premise that if a minister or a private Christian should drop an expression which not being so well cautioned as it ought to be, is by reason of its ambiguity capable of being explained in an unsound sense: that even in this case, it is most unjust and uncharitable to explain it in such a sense: granting we have sufficient means of knowing that this sense is contrary to the persons settled opinion.

3. I would premise that granting we know that a person has readily been in an error in judgment for some time. Yet if we know that he has retracted said error, 'tis most disingenuous to speak of him as if he still retained it, and to endeavor to make the World believe that it is still his opinion. As for instance, would it not have been highly injurious to have charged Augustine with any of his former errors after he had written his book of retractions?

These few particulars being premised which I think cannot but be granted; I proceed as I proposed to try the spirits.

[1.] Of the promoters of this present work. And in the doing of this I shall essay to try them. (1.) With respect to their doctrine. (2.) With respect to their manner of life. (3.) With respect to the effects their labors have produced.

1. I shall essay to try them with respect to their doctrine. This is one excellent mark by which Christians may distinguish between true and false teachers: and therefore we have it prescribed as a rule by which we may discern between the spirit of Christ and the spirit of Antichrist, in context. Let a person be seemingly never so sober & blameless in his walk, let him make never so high pretences to inspiration or doctrine revelation; yet if he bring any doctrine contrary to Godliness, or which is subversive of the genuine doctrines of the gospel, we are not to believe that the spirit by which he is acted is of God. Yea although he should show a sign or wonder, & they should come to pas; yet ought we not to believe him: because thereby the Lord our God doth try us, Deut. 13. 1, 2, 3. We are not so much as to receive him into our houses, neither to bid him God speed. But though he appeared like an angel, we are to hold him accursed, 2 John 10. ver. Gal. 1. 8. Now the doctrines which the promoters of his work teach, the apostle's creed, of the 39 articles of the Church of England, and of the Westminster concession of Faith. To these they often appeal for the truth of what they preach. More particularly these men are careful to teach and inculcate the great doctrine of original sin, in opposition to Pelagius, Arminius,

and their respective followers. That this sin has actually descended from Adam, the natural and federal head, to all his posterity proceeding from him by ordinary generation; that hereby the understanding is darkened, the will depraved, and the affections under the influence of a wrong bias, to that degree that they are utterly indisposed to any thing that is spiritually good; that man, as a sad consequence of the fall, has lost all power in things spiritual. This doctrine they insist upon, in order to humble the pride of man, to drive him out of himself, and convince him of his own emptiness? They teach likewise with due care the doctrine of the imputation of the righteousness of the second Adam, which is Jesus Christ, God equal and of the same substance with the father, in order to atone for the guilt and cleanse from the first Adam; that he must be made to sinners wisdom, righteousness, sanctification, and redemption; and that he is the Lord our righteousness, Jer. 23. 6. As also that this righteousness is apprehended and applied by faith alone, without the deeds of the law; that all works are and consequently all boasting is excluded; that though works have no part in our Justification, yet the faith which justifies it self is lively and operative; that which justifies itself in sight of the World by works, which purifies the soul from the pollution of sin, and influences the person who has it to bring forth the fruits of the new obedience. They teach likewise that this faith is the gift of God; that a man cannot believe by any inherent power of his own; and yet notwithstanding faith being our act and a commanded duty, we are to endeavor to believe; and with a due sense of our own insufficiency and a humble dependence upon God for strength, we are to strive to exert the vital act. As to conversion or regeneration, they hold this to be made good, before the fruit be so; that except a man undergo a supernatural change by the operation of the Holy Ghost upon his soul, or be born of water and of the spirit, he cannot enter into the Kingdom of God. And in as much as they find that man in his natural state is full of self conceit, that in his own opinion he is rich and increased in goods and stands in need of nothing, or as Job expresses it, that vain man would be wise, through he be born like the wild asses colt; they therefore in their preaching make use of the terrors of the law: they use the law, as God has appointed it to be used, which is a subserviency to the gospel, or as a schoolmaster to bring men to Christ, Gal. 3. 24. But to say that the law is the only topic on which they constantly insist, endeavoring to work on the lower passions, and to drive men with slavish fear like brute creatures, is false and slanderous. They preach also the consolations of the gospel, the intrinsic beauty of holiness, and the reasonableness of Christ's service. As to the spirit, I never heard that the most considerable promoters of this work pretended to the extraordinary gifts thereof that were peculiar to the apostolic age. I believe I might venture to challenge their adversaries to show that they pretend to the spirit in any other sense, than in his convincing, enlightening, directing and comforting influences. And in these respects the spirit is the privilege of all believers. If any man have not the spirit of Christ, thus, he is none of his Rom. 8. 10. As to civil government, they are exceeding loyal, they put men in mind to be subject to principalities and powers; to render all their dues, tribute to whom tribute is due, honor to whom honor, and fear to whom fear; to render to Cesar the things that are Cesar's; and to pray for Kings, and all in authority, that we may live quiet and peaceable lives in all godliness and honesty. With respect to the government of the church, they hold that Christ is the sole head and King of the Church; that the government is upon his shoulders; that he is the King of Kings and Lord of the Lords; that in order to the management of the affairs of his house, he has set officers in the same; that he has vested these, not with a legislative power, or a power to make new laws and impose them upon his free subjects, but only with an executive power, or power to put in execution those laws which he has already made. I might instance a great many other particulars with respect to the soundness of these men's doctrines; but the time would fail me: And therefore let it suffice to say, that their opposers have not been able to hitherto, and I believe cannot yet show one particular in which they have departed from the faith.

I am aware it may be said by some; but why do these men insist so much upon original sin, upon the new birth, and justification by faith alone? Are there not other doctrines to be preached as well as these? And is it not the business of a gospel minister to declare the whole counsel of God? To which I answer 1. That I deny that they always insist upon these particular doctrines. 2. I take these to be some of the reasons why they insist so much upon them. (1.) Because these are great important doctrines. Justification by faith (as Luther has observed) is the article of a standing or falling church. And indeed we cannot deny the observation of the just, if we allow what the apostle says, which is that if righteousness come by the law, Christ is dead in vain. (2.) Because it is exceedingly difficult to bring vain conceited man to a firm and steadfast belief of them. (3.) Another reason why they insist so little upon these doctrines is because others insist so little upon them: Nay, some do openly deny them; deny the necessity of supernatural grace, hold the power of man's will in things spiritual, say that we are justified partly by faith and partly by obedience, and that Christ's righteousness was only to make up the defects of our righteousness. It is not high time for all who are faithful to Christ's cause, to appear for and inculcate these doctrines, when Christ is thus wounded in the house of his professed friends? When the very foundations of our religion are shaken, and the distinguishing doctrines of Christianity are explained away? For this I may venture to say; that Arminianism tends to design, and design supersedes the Christian scheme: no need of Christ to do that which we are supposed to have power to do ourselves: If righteousness came by the law, then Christ is dead in vain.

2. Let us try them with respect to their manner of life. And can it be denied that this has been very exemplary and heavenly? I grant indeed, that this of itself is no proof of their being sent of God, if their doctrines were false. The character of Socinus was wise, grave, religious, &c. But when purity of the doctrine & life

go together; both unite make a very strong evidence. Now the most famous and successful of them do evidently appear to have much of their conversation in heaven, to have a great degree of knowledge of their own hearts. What a sweet forgiving spirit do they show to their most virulent and bitter enemies? What lambs are they in their own cause, and yet what lions in Christ's? We see an example of this with respect to Mr. Wesley and Mr. Whitefield: The latter of these had a most endeared affection for the former; and yet he, which is Wesley, had no sooner stricken at the great doctrines of election and the saints final perseverance, but the other appears openly against him: Thereby showing that the cause of Christ was dearer to him than any friend he had upon Earth, and he knew no man after the flesh, 2 Cor. 5. 16.

3. Let us try them with respect to their abundant labors. And have not several of them been eminent followers of Christ? In this particular how zealous are they about their master's business? How are these angels or messengers of God caused to fly swiftly in publishing the everlasting Gospel to them that dwell upon the Earth? What prodigious fatigue of body and mind do they expose themselves to, out of a tender love to souls? And how wondrously are they supported in all their toil? These things are so remarkable with respect to Mr. Whitefield in particular, that the great and pious Dr. Watts of London speaking of him in a letter to his correspondent here, expresses himself thus; "I must say it seems to me as though some divine power attended him to support him under such endless fatigues." In a word, I think these men may very consistent with modesty and truth appeal to the churches where they have been, and say with the apostle 2 Tim. 3. 10. But thou hast fully known my doctrine, manner of life, purpose, faith, long suffering, charity, patience.

4. Let us next try them with respect to the effects that their labors have produced, and can any have the front to deny that these have been good? Have not convetous worldlings in a great measure had their affections weaned from the things of the Earth,

and set upon those things that are above: Are there not innumerable instances of swearers, drunkards, unclean persons, tattlers, liars, Sabbath-breakers, &c. who have left off their favorite vices; have cut off the right hand, and plucked out the right eye? Have not several pharisaical self justifying persons, who thought themselves in a very good state before, had their sandy foundations discovered; so that they have been made to alter their tone, and instead of saying, God I thank thou that I am not as other men are, they have not many had their secret sins so particularly touched by the penetrating sword of God's spirit, that they have been made to cry, Lord be merciful to us sinners? Have not many had their secret sins so particularly touched by the penetrating sword of God's spirit, that they have been made to cry out with the woman of Samaria, come see a man that told me all that ever I did? Have not many seen both the heinousness of sin, and the desirableness of Christ, with other eyes that ever they did before? Have found a sweetness in the Bible, a delight in secret prayer, and Christian conference, and meditation, that before they were strangers to? Has not bigotry been very much subdued? And many of late have so learned Christ, as to esteem one another as Christians, and not to place the Kingdom of Heaven in meats and drinks? Yea, has not God in his just sovereignty been revealed the mysteries of his Kingdom to babes, while he has hid them from the wise and prudent? Have not little children been heard singing hosanna to the son of David? God thus perfecting praises from the mouth of babes and sucklings, and to the stilling of the enemy and the avenger. Oh my brethren, are any of you under the malignant influence of such a woeful prejudice, as to imagine that these and many other such desirable effects are the works of the Devil? It is my hope and shall be my prayer that God will remove your prejudices.

And thus I have endeavored to try the spirits that promote this work. Next let us try the spirits of the opposers of the same, and in doing this I shall endeavor to try them. (1.) With respect to their doctrine, (2.) With respect to the spirit of temper, with which they oppose the present work.

1. Let us try them with respect to their doctrine. And it will be found upon examination that some of the most violent opposers are men of Armenian, Pelagian, and Deistical principles. This is too evident to be denied: several of them being such as scoff at the imputation of original sin, who deny the doctrine of justification by faith alone, as likewise the high doctrine of predestination: and who do strongly assert man's natural powers in things spiritual. I foresee indeed that it may be said that all who oppose the present work are not men of such principles, granting some be, I answer, I charitably hope they are not: But I should rejoice that they would give less reason, to suspect them of verging that way. Is it not a truth too plain to be denied, that there has been of late a great growth of the subtitle error of Arminius in the Protestant World? And I wish I could say that our side of the Atlantic were free of it. Why then are they not more careful to preach against it, to tell their people of the danger of it, to show them that it is destructive to true Christianity. In a word, when they appear as zealous against it, and make as loud a cry concerning the danger of it, as they do against the new schemers as they affect to term them: We shall then have more room for charity towards them in this regard.

After all, I do charitably believe that there are some weaker brethren, both of ministers and people, who are led to oppose this work, and yet are no Armenians; but are found in the doctrines of predestination, supernatural grace, and justification by faith alone: But in the mean time, I believe that the principal and most inveterate opposers are men of Armenian and Pelagian principles, and that these others are only deputy or second hand opposers. They are like the two hundred men who went with Absalom from Jerusalem at the time of rebellion: But were not made privy to the plot? It is said of them that they in their simplicity and knew not any thing. As these are honest in the main; there is the better ground to hope that God in his good time will undeceive them, and let them see their error. And thus far with respect to their doctrine.

I come next to try them with respect to the spirit or temper with which they oppose the present work. I shall show a few of the properties of this spirit, which in an obvious manner do discover themselves in the opposers.

1. As many of them seem to be acted by a lying spirit. That same father of lies, who was a lying spirit in the mouth of Ahab's prophets, is still in being. And indeed if ever Hell seemed to be broken loose in horrid lies and calumny, now appears to be the time. I would not say that all who oppose the present work are willful liars because I would be as charitable as possible: but this seems to be the case; which is some hatch the lies, and others laboring under the malignant Influence of a prejudiced mind do too easily believe them and report them for truths. How else I pray comes it to pass that so many horrid lies are forged? Has not Mr. Whitefield been represented as a base, mercenary, convetous men, one who goes about gathering money to make an estate for himself? Have not both he and Messieurs the Erskin's Scotland been represented as persons in confederacy with the Pope, as employed by the man of sin to bring other people to the cursed errors of the Church of Rome? Have not several of their doctrines been grossly misrepresented, as any person may see who will read with candor what they have written in their own defense? Have not their ungraded expressions been laid hold of, yea words put upon the rack to export meanings from them which it is plain the authors never intended? Are there not some who are industrious in endeavoring to make people believe, that these men hold it as a principle, that a few tears and some convulsion like fits are of themselves sufficient evidences of a work of God? That they pretend to the gifts of discerning spirits to such a degree as to know whether a person be converted or not by looking in his face, or by a few words discourse with him? That all converted persons behoove to be able to give account of their conversion with respect to its time, manner, and other circumstances? But it would swell to a volume to repeat one half of the slander that is cast upon them. The same game is played against them, which was by the Church of Rome against our reformers from Popery,

and by the Scribes and Pharisees against our blessed Lord and his apostles. Now my brethren, say I beseech you what spirit these lies do proceed from: whither it is most probable that they come from God of truth or the father of lies. One would think a good cause did not need such props as these to support it.

2. As it is a lying so it is a most uncharitable spirit. The opposers of the present work do blame the promoters of the same for want of charity; because these preach (as they say) too much terror, and make the gate of Heaven too strait. But what I pray can be more uncharitable than to represent this whole work in a general undistinguished manner as the work of the Devil? To say it is nothing but fanaticism and enthusiasm? That it is like a bubble upon the water which will quickly be gone? That the men who promote it are wandering stars, or blazing comets, or like raging waves of the sea foaming out their own shame? Are these the gentlemen of such extensive charity! Is this the wisdom that cometh from above; which is pure, peaceable, gentle, easy to be entreated? This that charity described by the apostle, 1 Cor. 13? Which vaunteth not itself, doth not behave itself unseemly, which thinketh no Evil? If this be charity, let God deliver me from the effects of it! Oh my soul come not thou into their secret, into their assembly mine honor be not thou united. Gen. 49. 6.

3. As it is an uncharitable so it is an envious spirit. Envy is a most diabolical passion: This is thought to be one of the prime causes of the Devil's first rebellion against his creator. And it were to be wished that there was not one fiber of this cursed root in ministers. Alas, does not the conduct of some of them give too much ground to suspect that they envy the success of the Lord's work in the hands of their brethren. That which ought to be a matter of joy to them, seems to irritate their Spleen, and to fill them with a peevish discontent. Oh that such ministers had more of the spirit of Moses; who when he was told that Eldad and Medad prophesied in the camp and desired to forbid them, says to the messenger, enviest thou for my sake? Would to God that all

the Lord's people were prophets &c. Or that of John the Baptist; who rejoiced at the growing fame of Jesus, saying, he must increase, but I must decrease. Or that of Paul; who rejoiced that Christ was preached through by some out of envy and strife. O that ministers instead of weakening, would endeavor to strengthen each others hands; that they would rejoice in each others usefulness. Is not the harvest plenty? Are not the labors few? Is there not work enough for all in the spacious vineyard of Christ? Why need they than stand quarreling with one another; when there is so much planting, watering, pruning and cultivating to be done?

4. As it is an envious, so it is a partial spirit. The apostle James gives it as one of the properties of the wisdom that cometh from above, that it is without partiality. There is no perfection in this corrupt sinful state. Many blemishes are to be seen in the life of the most eminent saint; which are the inevitable consequents of human frailty and remains of a body of sin and death. So that if all the defects of any author, all the blemishes of any person, all the imprudencies in the management of any cause be industriously gathered together and magnified, and in the mean time no mention made of that which is commendable in them; it will make the best person or cause in the World look with a dark and gloomy aspect. As for instance look into the life of David the man after God's own heart. Gather all the blemishes thereof together, his lying, his vain glory, his cruelty, his murder, his adultery; and in the mean time, suffer partiality to draw a vail over the bright part of his character, which shall conceal whatsoever was excellent in him. And this picture of him so drawn, shall be so far from amiable, that it will look monstrous and deformed.

Now I appeal to facts, whither this be not the practice of many of the opposers of the present work? They constantly pore upon the dark side of it: whatever they can hear of that, they imagine will cast a slur upon it; they greedily lay hold of, and magnify with all their art and eloquence. If a friend of the work be imprudent, or unguarded in any part of his conduct; this shall be industriously improved, but not a word said of what is commendable in him. If he drop an expression that is somewhat ambiguous, they will be sure to interpret it in the worst sense. Nor do they stop here, but give out that this is the opinion of the whole party. I appeal to the unprejudiced, whither this be candid, impartial treatment?

5. Lastly, as it is a partial so it is a profane mocking spirit. I am grieved at heart that I have occasion to mention this. But let any man peruse the writings of Commissary Garden in Carolina, and compare these with some ludicrous sarcastical language that is vented in other places, both from press and pulpit, and then say whether this be a false charge. Felix trembled when Paul reasoned of righteousness, of temperance and judgment to come. Soul concern had the same effect upon the jailor, Acts 16. Peter's hearers felt the dint of the gospel two edge sword, so as to be pricked at the heart, Act. 2. The father of the child cried out with tears, saying, Lord I believe, help mine unbelief: Mark 5. 24. God speaking of true penitents, says, he will lead them with weeping and supplication, Jer. 31. 9. The Psalmists heart trembled before God, and he was afraid of his righteous judgments. Heman while he suffered the terrors of the Lord, was distracted. Psal. 88. 14. God's people are said to be persons of pure lip, Zeph. 3. 7. And to speak the language of Canaan, Isai. 17. 18. The Psalmist says, Oh taste and see that the Lord is good, Psal. 34. and elsewhere, come and hear all ye that fear God; I will tell you what he hath done for my soul. We read, Mal. 3. 16. That those who feared the Lord spoke often one to another. What did they speak of? Why did they discoursed of God's mercy, justice, holiness, patience, and wisdom, evidenced in the government of the World. They established each other in the ways of God against the proud and atheistical disputers of those days. But now in our days when God's word and spirit produced the same effects which those mentioned in the above quoted texts; these things are all vilified, and undervalued. Man are made to believe that there is no need of tears and deep sorrow for sin; the work of conversion may be done in a more smooth, rational and easy way; that these are no probable symptoms of a work of God; they may be all

accounted for from physical and mechanical principles. Persons must not entertain religious conversation, use mutual freedom in talking over their experiences and communing about the state of their souls; this savors too much of hypocritical ostentation, and is inconsistent with decency and politeness. By this means, alas. Alas, the bruised reed is broken and the smoking flax quenched; men are rocked asleep in the cradle of carnal security; and instead of being put upon soul enquiry, they are made to believe that they are well enough already. So that they go smoothly down the stream to Hell, singing Agag's Requiem to themselves, that surely the bitterness of death is already past. Oh that God would give such ministers to see what they are doing; whose interest they are serving, while they are filling the minds of poor people with groundless prejudices against the work of God.

And thus I have endeavored to bring the spirits, first of the promoters, second of the opposers of the present work to the rule or standard. And having so done, I desire everyone to judge for himself, and to say which appears to be most of God, which endures best to be weighed in the balance of the sanctuary.

I proceed now to the improvement: and thou the subject would naturally afford several useful inferences; yet in regard I'm afraid I have already incurred the censure of tediousness, I shall pass other uses of the same, and conclude with some words of exhortation. In which I shall apply myself first to all in general; and second to several sorts of persons, according to their different circumstances.

First to all in general; I would say my dear brethren; take the wholesome advise of the apostle in my text; i.e. not to believe every spirit; but try the spirits whether they be of God. Do not implicitly pin your faith upon any man's sleeve. Be followers of no man farther than he is of Christ. To what end has God made you reasonable creatures, and given you the Bible in your mother tongue, but that you should judge for yourselves? Make use therefore of your Christian liberty. Bring persons, their doctrines, their spirit, and their practices, to the law and to the testimony.

And as they agree or disagree herewith, receive or reject them. Be exceedingly careful that party prejudice don't bias your judgment. This is exceedingly dangerous; especially when it is in soul affairs. Oh let me plead with you to be faithful to your precious souls. Lay aside all prejudice of every kind, whether religious, national, congregational, domestic, or personal. Hang out the balance fairly, and let the word of God be judge. Be importunate with God, that he would give you a right sight of yourselves, that he would show your souls state whatever it be, whether good or bad. You'll never be able to try the spirits of others as well, until you have tried your own spirits. Alas, how many are forward in judging others, who know not what spirit themselves are of? Pull the beam out of your own eye, and then you'll see the better to pull the mote out of your brothers.

But Secondly, I would be more particular in applying myself to several sorts of persons, according to their different circumstances.

And 1. To you who are full of strong prejudices against this work; insomuch that you are inclinable to think that it is all delusion, and the work of the Devil. I would ask you; were not some of you very warm in favor of it within these twelve months? What of the reason of your sudden change? Have you discovered that the promoters of this work have vented any false doctrine, or been guilty of any wicked practice since that time? I would ask you farther: have you not at some times a hesitating or doubting in your minds about this work? Granting you be not fully satisfied that it is of God, yet certainly you cannot say you are sure that it is not of God. Don't you feel somewhat within you saying at times, possibly I am mistaken; perhaps this work is from heaven? Is this the case with some of you? Than I would entreat you not to show yourselves virulent opposers of it. See that you make not conversion-work the subject of your common drollery and division. Have a care of talking lightly concerning tears and sorrow for sin. Consider that if the work be of God, as you do not know but it is; than by this sort of conduct you'll be found fighting against God, and grieving the blessed spirit. Be not mockers then, least your bands be made strong, Isa. 28. 22. I appeal to your consciences; have any of you already been guilty of this sort of conduct, yet despair not? There is hope in Israel concerning you. You will with Saul the persecutor obtain mercy, because you did it ignorantly and in unbelief. But if conscience duly informed tells you that it is God's work, and yet you do willfully and maliciously go on to ridicule and oppose it; assure yourselves that this is a doing despite to the spirit of grace. This is sinning against the Holy Ghost? "Tis an audacious shooting of the arrows of your scorn directly against the throne of the great and dreadful God! Oh then be exhorted to stop in time. Tremble do you think what you are doing: Beg that God would keep you back from presumptuous sin. Take care, if you be in doubt about the work, to have conscience duly informed. Try both sides, and then you'll be the more capable to form an impartial judgment. Prove all things, and hold fast that which is good; 1. Thess. 5. 21. My dear brethren, what should make any of you to doubt concerning the work's being of God? Will you but judge of the tree by it's fruit? Is it the work of the Devil to make men who were at ease in Zion careful about their souls? To set them about secret prayer, self-expression, and Christian conference? To wean their affections from the World, and to set their desires more upon Heaven? To give them a sight of the vileness of their own hearts, and thereby to humble their natural pride? To make sin appear exceedingly sinful, and Christ exceedingly precious in their eyes? Is it the Devils work to make swearers, whores, drunkards, liars, Sabbath breakers, scoffers at religion, to leave off their respective vices? Let me entreat you to weigh these particulars with that care which an affair of the last consequence deserves. What interest do you imagine I can propose to myself in using this freedom with you, but a tender concern for your souls? I am looking for nothing from you; I propose no temporal gain by you. Oh then if you do not regard me, regard your own precious souls.

But then I would next apply myself to you who are professed favorites of the present work. And of you I imagine there are two sorts, i.e. graceless and gracious persons. A World to each of you.

(1.) You have no saving experience of religion upon your souls, never yet have seen either your misery or the need of the remedy. Poor souls! Alas what will it avail you that you are professedly on the Lord's side and seemingly very warm in the cause, crying with Jebu, come see my zeal for the Lord of hosts? If your heart be not right with God, your being among good company will be no more benefit to you than it was to Judas. What are you trusting to? Is it your baptism, your visible Church membership, your speculative or head-knowledge, your soundness and orthodoxy on principle? I tell you through these things must be, yet of themselves they will never do. You may have all these, and yet if you go no further, you'll certainly be damned. Think not then to say within yourselves we have Abraham to our father. Trust not to lying words, saying, the temple of the Lord, the temple of the Lord. Or are you trusting to your convictions? Is it the ground of your confidence that you have shed a few tears and can remember the time when you were under some concern? Remember that this of itself will not do; that Felix trembled, the sinners in Zion were afraid, Isa. 33. 14. That Esau shed tears, and yet was no true penitent. Your hearts must be changed; your affections must be turned into another channel? Yea the prevailing bent and temper of your souls must be quite altered. In a word, you must become new creatures, 2 Cor. 5. 17.

But then last of all to you who are not only warm in this good cause, but are so from a right principle. I would say to you my dear brethren; that I hope there are none of you in any measure shaken by the opposition that God's work meets with you in various places. Certainly you have no reason. I can appeal to you, whether those who may be looked upon as the most considerable promoters of the present work have been bringing any new doctrines to your ears, with respect to the nature of conversion, or with respect to the operations of the blessed spirit, or with respect to assurance of grace; or in any one particular, but what are the doctrines of your Bibles, of your confession of faith, and catechisms; the doctrines which your dear ancestors died in, and which some of them sealed with their blood. Don't then suffer your selves to be bantered out of your senses by a loud cry of error and heresy breaking in upon the Church; when you cannot but know that it is a false alarm. And if you would not be soon shaken in mind; be always laboring after greater degrees of knowledge, to be better rooted in your principles, to arrive at the stature of adult men in Christianity, who have their senses exercised to know both good and evil. Hold fast the profession of your faith without wavering; that you be not henceforth children, tossed to and fro and carried about with every wind of doctrine. And, my dear brethren, let me in particular exhort you to keep up heart work, and to maintain spiritual communion with God. Watch and pray that ye enter not into temptation. Remember that though you are not the Devil's subjects, that you are still in his territories, and therefore liable to his assaults. Be careful to exercise the Christian grace of charity. Don't be guilty of rash judging. Remember that your Lord has said, judge not that you be judged. See that you condemn not all that differ from you in judgment about the present work, as carnal, graceless and enemies of God. Consider that even a good man may be a while in an error. This I charitably believe is the case with some in the land at this day. See that you guard against a litigious, wrangling temper. Don't be forward upon all occasions to enter into disputes with the opposers of the work. Such a humor, if it prevail, will have a mischievous tendency insensibly to worm out practical religion. Rather then, choose to convince your opposers by your lives. Let your light shine before men, that they may see your good works. If they say you are proud, convince them that it is false, by your humility. If they say you are uncharitable, contentious, show them that it is not so, by your peaceable conduct. Show by these means that your religion is more than an empty name; having a powerful influence on your practice. That the grace of God which has appeared unto you bringing salvation, has taught you to deny ungodliness and all worldly lusts, and to live soberly righteously and godly in the present World. If thus my brethren you conduct yourselves, God will say to you as he did to the Church in Philadelphia, Revel. 3. 8. 10. Thou hast a little strength, and hast kept my word, and hast not denied my name. Because thou hast kept the word of my patience; I also will keep thee from the hour of temptation which cometh upon the World, to try them that dwell upon the Earth.

F I N I S.

Professors Warned
OF THEIR
DANGER.
A
SERMON
FROM
MATTH. iii. 9, 10.
Preach'd at Stratham,
DECEMBER 28, 1741

By the Reverend
Mr. *David McGregore*
of *Londonderry* in *New-England*

Published at the Request of the hearers.

BOSTON, in *NEW-ENGLAND*

Printed and Sold by J. Draper, in Newbury Street
1742.

Professors

Warn'd of their

DANGER.

MATTH III. ix. x.

And think to say within yourselves, we have Abraham to our father for I say unto you that God is able of these stones to raise up children to Abraham. And now also the axe is laid to the root of the trees, therefore every tree which bringeth not forth good fruit is hewn down and cast into the fire.

E read, Matth. 21. 28. &c. that our savior speaks a parable to the Pharisees concerning a certain man who had two sons, and he said to the first, "Go, work today in the vineyard", who answered his father, "I will not", but afterwards he repented and went. And he came to the second and said likewise; and he answered, "I go sir" but went not. Upon which our savior puts the question to them, wither of them twain, did the will of his father? They answered, him, the first. Whereupon our Lord makes particular application of the parable to them, and expressly tells them, that the publications and harlots should enter into the Kingdom of Heaven before them. And

indeed it is so. Persons who have somewhat of a religious education, if they be destitute of the grace of God, and strangers to vital experimental religion, are generally the hardest to work upon of any of mankind. The reason why they are so is obvious; because they esteem themselves well enough already. They are rich and increased with goods, and stand in need of nothing. Tell them of the necessity of faith; why they know it. But why do you tell them of it? They are believers already, they have been baptized in their infancy, have been bred up in the sound orthodox faith, have a speculative knowledge, being instructed out of the law. So that none is more ready than they are, externally to approve of the things that are excellent. They have been catechized and instructed in the principles of religion from their childhood; they have heard and read many excellent sermons; have often sat at the Lord's Table; they have eat and drink in the presence of Christ, and he hath taught in their streets: so that there is no danger of them. Thus alas! They rest in the outside of religion, and satisfy themselves with a name to live. Insomuch that Hell is filling fast with knowing civil, moral hypocrites. I make no great question that there are some of these in every Christian congregation. O! That I could do anything that might be instrumental in discovering to them their sandy foundations, and showing them their rotten insides! That I could make them sensible how far they are outstripped by those who they count their inferiors in religion. That so (as the apostle says, Rom. 11. 14.) I might by any means provoke them to emulation, and might save some of them! What a desirable sight would it be, to see such old Pharisees barren from all their false confidences, driven out of themselves and drawn unto Christ! To behold them in the most humble manner falling down at the footstool of sovereign grace, and crying, mercy, mercy! Although this be a difficult work, yet I am certain that the Devine power can accomplish it, and that there is nothing too hard for God. That I may therefore have an opportunity of speaking somewhat suitable to their case, I have chosen the words of the Baptist as the subject of the ensuing discourse; where he is professedly dealing with such persons; and indeed he does very plainly, when he says in the context, Oh Generation of vipers, who hath warned you to fly from the wrath to come? But then follows the words of my text, in which we have these two particulars noticeable. First, we have the ground of their false confidence detected. Secondly, we have their danger plainly honestly laid before them.

First, we have the ground of their false confidence detected in these words; think not to say within yourselves, we have Abraham to our father. Every person who has present ease has certainly something that he relies upon; were wicked men sensible of what their true state is, it would be impossible that they should have one moments ease. They therefore have something by which they make a shift to quiet conscience for the present. Something that makes them imagine they have a covenant with death, and an agreement with Hell, which emboldens them to say, we shall have peace, though we walk after the imaginations of our own hearts. Some have one ground of confidence, and some another. This was the ground of the Jews confidence they knew that God had made an everlasting covenant with Abraham to be the God of him and his seed, Gen. 17. 2, 3, 4. They knew likewise that they were his descendants by natural generation or his seed after the flesh. Hence they concluded they were in a safe condition that they were God's people and he was their God. The Baptist who was a plain, honest minister of Christ, does in faithfulness to his master, and love to their souls, show them the vanity of their confidence. It is as if he said, "I know what you trust to: you think that as you are the only visible Church in the World, should you be destroyed, God would have none to show mercy to, and with whom he might keep that everlasting covenant made with Abraham." But mistake not yourselves; those only are the children of Abraham, that do the works of Abraham; although you are Abraham's children by natural generation, yet by your original corruption and your actual transgressions, you are the children of the Devil, so that if there were no more men and women upon the Earth but your petty nation, yet before God would bestow upon you the covenant blessings of faithful Abraham, while you continue in your present impenitent state, he would raise up children to Abraham out of the stones.

But then the second thing in the World is their danger. This plainly laid before them in these words, and now also the axe is laid to the root of the tree, every tree, &c. Some divines are of opinion that this is a prediction of the terrible destruction that a few years afterwards came upon the City of Jerusalem, and the whole commonwealth of the Jews, by Vespasian the Roman Emperor, and Titus his Son. However this may be, the plain sense is this, which is that if they repented not, they should feel the weight of the divine wrath. It is as if he had said "You had need to look about you and turn speedily from your sins to the living God, e're it be too late: God will be so far from sparing you because you are Abrahams children and his professing people, that he will cause judgment to commence at the house of God. 1 Pet. 4. 17. He will command the destroying Angel to begin at his sanctuary, Ezek. 9. 6. It is therefore high time for you to bestir yourselves, inasmuch as at this present time judgment is as nigh to be executed upon you as the tree is to falling, when the Axe is actually applied to the root of it."

I shall only improve the first part of the words now explained in a doctrine manner. And from then I take occasion to make this observation.

DOCTRINE

That men who live within the pale of the visible Church, are exceedingly prone to that dangerous sin of relying upon their outward advantages and performances, while in the mean time they are entire strangers to anything of vital experimental religion.

HAT it was so in the days of John Baptist, is evident from the words of my text; that it was so in the days of Jeremiah, is plain from Jer. 7. 4. Trust me not to lying words, saying, the temple of the Lord, the temple of the Lord, &c. The Jews thought they were certainly a happy people, because they had the symbols of the divine presence, and especially they were went proudly to boast of their temple, as if hereby the presence of God were in a manner chained to them. The prophet shows them that this was a trusting to lying words and warns them of the danger. That it was so in the days of our savior is evident from several of his reasonings with Jews. This was the case of the Church of Laodicea, Rev. 3. 17. She thought she was rich and increased with goods, and stood in need of nothing. And that this is the temper of great many professors to this day is too evident to need proof.

The method in which I design to prosecute this subject shall be as follows;

First I shall endeavor to show some of those false foundations upon which professors are apt to build; and thence groundlessly to conclude that their state is good.

Secondly, I shall propose a few close experimental questions to them; if possible, to convince them that the main thing is yet lacking with them, and that they must go a greater length than yet they have gone, or else perish eternally. And then make application.

I begin with the first of these, which is to show some of those false grounds upon which professors are apt to build, and by this means miserably to deceive and ruin their own poor souls.

And, first one ground of the presumptions confidences of such persons is, their Church privileges. Such are apt to pity the pagan World, and to say, "Alas for the poor heathens! They are indeed a very lamentable condition; they have no knowledge of the history of man's fall, of the sad consequences of that fall, nor of the way that God has revealed to lift up man from his fallen state. They never heard of the doctrine of Trinity, nor of the substantial union of the divine and humane natures in the wonderful and adorable person of our Immanuel. In a word, they are destitute of all the great and excellent privileges of our gospel, and taken captive by Satan at his will.

But as for us (say they) we are in an excellent state; we live in a land of vision; we have God's word and ordinances; we have been baptized in our infancy; and ever since, we have had the privileges of God's covenanted people, we have sat under the droppings of the gospel; we have eat and drank in the presence of Christ, and he hath taught in our streets; and therefore we may conclude that we are safe" Thus poor gospel sinners do deceive themselves; not considering that they may have all these outward privileges, yea with Capernaum be lifted up to Heaven in them, and yet are liable to be cast down into the lowest pit in Hell; that he is not a Jew that is one outwardly, neither is that circumcision that is outward in the flesh; that 'tis not everyone that cries, Lord! Lord! That shall enter into the Kingdom of Heaven. My fellow professors, I wish this may not be the case with many of you; if it be, your privileges will only serve to enhance your guilt and misery, and to make your Hell the hotter. Oh we have reason to think that many a poor gospel sinner is now roaring in Hell, who wishes that he had been born at the Cape of Good Hope, among the Hottentots, rather than to have lived to abuse gospel light!

Secondly, another ground of such persons false confidence is, their knowledge. They are well acquainted with the speculative part of religion; so that they can talk upon several points of divinity, with a good deal of justness of thought and pertinency of expression. They have theoretic knowledge of the scripture, so that they may be able to quote it with promptness and repeat it with fluency; yea they may have a kind of love to talk of things divine (especially upon controverted points) from a principal of vain-glory and that they may have an opportunity of discovering their parts. They may have God near in their mouths while he is far from their reins; and the same principle may lead them to several acts that are materially good. They may for instance, be the foremost in meetings for fasting and prayer; thus the Pharisees to whom John is speaking in my text, fasted often; and made many long prayers. They may visit the sick; may talk of the decay of religion; may pray for the day of the Lord, and for the down-pouring of the spirit. In a word, they may have a great deal of knowledge in their head, while they have no grace in their hearts. This was the state of the Pharisees; and I would have every one of you, Oh professors, to examine that it be not your case; see that you know yourselves; labor for a mere intimate acquaintance with your own hearts; take heed that your knowledge be not a barren speculative knowledge, all confined to your head; and that your love to Christ be not wholly in the World and in tongue; if it be, I will tell you, you know nothing yet as you ought to know. I'm persuaded the Devil knows more than the most knowing of you, and yet I hope none will say he has any true grace. See John 3. 17.

Thirdly, another false ground of such person's confidence is their outward duties. They are sensible that God has instituted some particular duties to be practiced by his professing people; they know likewise that their practice agrees with the divine institution; and hence they conclude themselves in a good state.

But alas! they consider not that God has said my son give me thy heart. They don't take narrow notice of themselves, to see whether they be leaning upon or trusting to these duties, instead of leaning upon Christ. We may imagine we hear them reasoning with themselves after this manner, "The more profane and negligent part of mankind are indeed in a very sad condition; they mind nothing of religion; they seldom attend sermons or sacraments; they don't pray in their families; or in their closets; there is not a World of religious conversation to be heard out of their mouths, more than if they had not souls. But as for me I cannot charge myself with such a conduct; I have been a punctual attender upon ordinance; I have prayed in my family; and sometimes I have been at secret prayer in my closet; and when any religious conversation has been introduced, I have been as ready as many in company to bear my part in it." Examine, oh professor, whether these are your pleas; are these all the ground of your confidence? I tell you if it be so, you are but almost Christians; you have got no further than the foolish virgins, for these carried a lamp of profession and went the whole round of duty; and you may go confidently up to the Gate of Heaven as they did, saying, Open to us Lord! But the judge will say to you as to them, I know you not.

Fourthly, another ground of such persons false confidence is, their soundness in the principles of religion. They have kept the ordinances as they are delivered to them in the sacred oracles of divine truth; they can readily assent to every article of the creed; they can, without hesitation, give an explicit assent to the approved standards of the Churches, whereof they are members. This was the case of the self confident persons, with whom the apostle expostulates, Rom. 2. 17, 18. Behold thou art called a Jew, and resteth in the law, and make thy boast of God. And knowest his will, and approvest of the things that are most excellent, being I structed out of the law, and art confident that thou, &c. Such an one may hear Petagian, Arminian and Pharisaical principles refuted with pleasure; he may go along with the preacher when he is teaching of these points, and with a secret complaisance approved of everything he says, and yet he may be a selfjointifying Arminien, or a proud Pharisee all the while. Imagine I hear some person say, "I'm sure this is not my case, I know that original sin is descended from Adam, the natural and covenant head to all his posterity; I know that man has no power of will since the fall to do anything spiritually good that in order hereunto, it is God that must work in him to will and to do; that all my righteousness is like filthy rags that the best of my performances, cannot recommend me to God; that by the deeds of the law, no flesh living can be justified; and that without Christ, I can do nothing; I know that a man must be born of water and of the spirit; that he must be converted and become as a little child, otherwise he cannot enter into the Kingdom of Heaven; and therefore, I am sure I am no Pharisee nor Arminian." But then, I would ask you who are thus confident. (and I would pray you to be faithful to your own souls in your answer) How do you know these things? Have you a practical knowledge, a heart or experimental sense of them? Do you find in the exercise of a Christian life, the necessity of continual supplies from Christ, as really as the branch has need of union with the root? Do you find by experience, that through Christ strengthening you, you can do all things? That you are weak when he withdraws his presence, and strong when he vouchsafes his assistance? Can you indeed say, that you not only believe , but that you see that every duty is tainted and polluted as it proceeds from you Or do you know these things only because you have been taught them from the pulpit, or have learned them in your Catechisms, or read them in your Bibles? While in the mean time you have no feeling sense of them; can't set to your seal that you know them to be true from your personal experience? Is this the case with you (as I doubt it is with many) then I must tell you, that you are Pharisees, Arminians, notwithstanding your denying the charge; your heads are right but your hearts are wrong; you are speculatively sound; but practically you are in a pernicious error.

Fifthly, another dangerous ground of such person's false confidence is, their civility and outward sobriety. They compare themselves with others and because they are not so bad as these, therefore they conclude that their state is good. They are apt to look among the more profane and licentious part of mankind, and then they bless themselves and say, "Lord! What wretched profligate creatures are these; hear how they swear, how they blaspheme, how they are not afraid to set their mouths against the Heavens; do but observe them how they lie, how they talk obscenely, how they scoff at religion, burlesque the scripture, and laugh at the shaking of God's spear—Behold, how they sit in taverns, instead of going to hear the word of God, 'till they drown the reason with strong drink to such a degree, that they are more like Brutes than men; how they indulge themselves in chambering and wantonness, and wallow like filthy swine in all the obscene and impure gratifications of sense. Behold others, how they cheat and over reach, as if they cared not that they sold their souls to the Devil for a schilling, or had forgotten that there is a supreme court of appeal a coming, where they will be obliged to give an account of the hidden things of dishonesty, which shall then be brought to light. I thank God, I cannot charge myself with these things, and therefore I may conclude that my state is good." But then I would ask you, is this all the ground of your confidence, which really amounts to no more than this, that you are not so bad as others? Is this what you trust to? Then you may assure yourselves, that you'll go to Hell as certainly as the profane. If your heart be only swept and garnished by an outward reformation, and in the mean time empty of Christ, then see your dreadful end, Matth, 12. 44. Nay, there is one consideration, which ought to be exceedingly shocking to you, which is this, which is that there is a great probability of convictions reaching these openly profane persons, and their proving sincere converts, than there is of reaching you who are more smooth and civil. If you are trusting in your smoothness and civility, the publicans and harlots shall enter into the Kingdom of Heaven before you, Matth. 21. 31. See to this purpose the parable, Luke 18. 11. Two men went up unto the

Temple to pray, &c. How vastly different were the dispositions of those two men? The Pharisee thought he was in an excellent condition, because he fasted so often and did so many good works. He spoke in such a strain as if he had thought God were beholden to him, rather than he to God. He looks down upon the poor publican with an eye of indignation and proud disdain; and thank God that he was not such a one. O had he got a fight of his own heart, so as to be sensible of the sink of abominable pollution that was there, he would quickly have altered his tone! It is very hard to reach those persons who are thus full of devilish pride. The poor publican had indeed been a vile sinner; but then he was sensible of his sins; he was cut to the heart at the thoughts of it; his mouth was stopped; he had not one word to say in his own vindication. It was impossible for the Pharisee to have a more contemptible opinion of him than he had of himself; he stood at a distance, was so weighed down with the sense of the heavy burden of sin, that he scarcely dared to lift up his eyes, but cried, Lord, be merciful to me a sinner. And mark the event, This man went down to his house justified rather than the other; and the reason is subjoined; for everyone that exalters himself shall be abased; and he that humbleth himself, shall be exalted. My brother, you had need to take heed that the Pharisees case be not yours; that you be not trusting to your civility, and a few moral duties, while you have never seen the pollution or plague of your own hearts, if this be your case. I can tell you that some of the vilest sinners will get pardon, while you with all your civility and morality, will go to Hell.

Sixthly, another dangerous ground of such persons false confidence is, their mistaking conviction for conversion, I believe this proves the ruin of many souls. Such a one may say, "I am none of those upon whom the gospel has never had any impression. I can remember the time when my heart was melted, and I had joy in hearing the word and in other ordinances: God's word was not a burden to me, but I took delight in approaching unto God. I can remember the time when I had great terror;

when the sense of God's anger and the awful prospect of a future judgment, made me tremble; and therefore I have reason to believe, that the word of God had a saving effect upon my soul." Thus alas, many poor souls miserably deceive themselves; their trembling was only like that of Felix, or like a fit of ague which was soon over. Their joy was not caused by a love of holiness, as such; but merely from a prospect of Heaven which they had never any true notion of. Their consciences were only half awakened; and therefore are fallen asleep again more securely than they were before. In a word, they have never seen Jesus; they have rested short of Christ, and are putting their repentance, tears, their sadden fits of joy and sorrow in this room. If they would look into their own hearts, they would see that the bent of them is the same as it was before; that the current of their lives is the same; that their affections are not yet turned into a new channel; that they have not yet learned to walk with God, and to mind the things of the spirit. But alas! They never consider these things, and thus they miserably deceive themselves.

Seventhly, another ground of such persons confidences is their party zeal. They know that lukewarmness is a temper most detectable to God. That he abhors a Gallio-like indifference, and that he has threatened to spew such out of his mouth. And then, when they look into themselves, they find they have zeal, and therefore they conclude that they are in a good condition, without ever considering the object, the grounds and motives of zeal. A person may be mighty zealous about religion, and yet his heart not be right with God; as in the example of Jebu, who said, come see my zeal for the lord of bests. Who more zealous than Paul, while a Pharisee? He verily thought in himself that it behooved him to do much against the name of Jesus of Nazareth. Thus the Jews were exceedingly zealous for their law and their Temple. The apostle bears them witness, that they had a zeal for God, but not according to knowledge, Roman 10. 2. Nay, what it but a blind zeal that excited them persecute the dear servants of God? John 10. 2. The time comet, that whosoever killeth you, will think that he doeth good service. Oh! It is a dreadful thing to be under the influence of such a blind party-zeal! And yet we have great reason to fear, that there are too many ignorant party-zealots among professors. They will make a loud outcry concerning the decay of religion and abounding of wickedness; they are willing to expend their substance, and even to venture their lives, for their own party or persuasion; and yet examine them nearly, and you will find too much reason to suspect that they are four uncharitable bigots; and that they are utter strangers to the wisdom that cometh from above. Men would do well to examine themselves with respect to their zeal by some such questions as these, "Oh my soul! Which sort of zeal is mine? Is it excited by a single view to glory of God, or am I zealous only to be seen of men, or from other sinister view? Is my zeal for Christianity in general, or is it confined to party? Is it exercised about the great things of the gospel, or is it about meats and drinks, i.e. things that are of a minute and circumstantial nature? Don't my zeal make me too remiss in the great and weighty parts of the law, while I busily engaged in tything mint, annis and cummin? Don't this zeal of mine make me an adversary to, and rigid against these whom I have reason to believe are the beloved children of God?" If men would thus carefully examine them many would find that gave no ground to build so much upon their zeal as they do.

And thus I have endeavored to show to show some of these fallacious grounds upon which mere nominal Christians are apt to build, and by this means to deceive their own poor souls.

I proceed next to the second general head, which is to propose a few close experimental questions to such professors; if possible to convince them that the main thing is yet lacking, and that they must go a greater length than they have yet gone, or else perish eternally.

In the former head I have endeavored to convince carnal professors that they build upon a wrong foundation; by these queries I would endeavor to let them see that they want the right foundation. And these may be comfortable to the saints, while they find in themselves those things which are a solid ground of hope.

And first, I would enquire of you who are professors, have you ever been convicted of sin? This is certainly necessary in all who come to Christ, as a preparative to their coming aright. Hence we are told, that our Lord came not to call the righteous, but sinners to repentance; i.e. such sinners as are sensible of sin, Matthew 9. 13. Hence, the spirit, when he cometh into the World, is said to convince or reprove the World of sin, John 16. 8. I don't mean, when I ask you this question, whether you are convinced in your judgment that sin is an evil: but, have you had a practical, heart affecting and realizing sense of sin? Have you discovered the bitter root, which is original sin? Have you been laboring and heavy laden? Have you been made to groan under sin, as a heavy burden, and to cry, oh wretched man that I am, &c? Do you not only believe that sin is an evil; but do you see and feel it to be so? And, has it been your earnest desire and prayer to God, that you might see more of the evil of sin, that so your hatred of it might be greater and your repentance more bitter?

But then, secondly I would enquire, what effects has this conviction of sin produced in you? Has it made you plainly to see your self in the state of a condemned criminal, exposed to the wrath of a holy and sin revenging God? Have you seen the sword of divine justice in the hand of an angry and sin revenging God; the terrible avenger of blood, ready to smite you? Have you heard the awful voice of the law, saying, cursed be everyone that continues not in all the statutes and ordinances that are written in the book of the law, to do them? And have you, upon this sense of your state, seen the absolute necessity of Jesus Christ; that every other way of salvation but this, is hedged up; that there is no other name under Heaven given among men whereby you can be saved? And farther, have you hereupon resolved to renounce self, in all it's forms, modes and interests; your natural, moral and religious self, that you might go to Christ quite empty and naked, in the Quality of guilty, condemned criminals, who deserve nothing but the wrath and curse of an angry God?

But then, I would not be understood as if I asserted, that the conviction of all persons operated exactly alike; either with respect to their degree or duration: I am sensible there is a great difference in this respect. This may, in part, be accounted for from the different ages, sexes, and complexion of persons; and the sort of lives they have lived, previous to their souls besides God's way in the sea; his judgments are deep; and his footsteps are hid. Some persons are more driven with terror; some are drawn with the silken cords of love; and some are sanctified as it were from the womb. But this I say, that thing itself must be done, however the manner of doing it would be various upon different subjects. And if we will enquire particularly into the cases of those, who, in the judgment of charity, we have reason to believe are effectually wrought upon, we shall find, that though there are several more minute circumstances wherein they differ, yet in the main things, they all agree; they have all the same sensations; there is a desirable identity of symptoms among them, as one face answers to another in a glass.

Thirdly, I would farther ask you, whether you have endeavored unfeignedly to accept of Christ upon the terms of the gospel? Have you taken in all his offices, as your Instructor and law-giver, as well as your savior? And farther, does your faith work by love? Can you say, that Christ is infinitely precious to you? That you can see him with other eyes than you did? That the sense of the wretched state you were in some time ago, and the happy deliverance you have met with, causes your heart to overflow with love and gratitude, and your very soul to cleave to your deliverer? So that you love his ministers, love his people, love his laws, his ordinances and his example? That you love holiness, because he loves it? Yea, that you love his cross; count it all joy when you fall into diverse temptations? And rejoice that you are counted worthy to suffer shame for his name? Don't you find, that a crucified Christ is the sweetest subject of meditation and discourse to you? That the language of your soul is, none but Christ, none but Christ? And that you determine not to know anything so much as Jesus Christ, and him crucified? That you don't love father, or mother, or brethren, or sisters, or any Earthly enjoyment so much, but that, by his grace, you would be willing to part with all for Christ; esteeming his reproaches greater riches than the treasures of Egypt.

Fourthly, with respect to the prevailing bent and temper of your souls; do you find, upon the best examination you are capable of making, that the new birth manifesting itself in its sweet effects upon your souls? That you are indeed become new creatures? That the change is begun in all the powers of your soul? That your blind understandings are enlightened; or as the apostle expresses it, Col. 3. 10. Renewed in knowledge, after the image of him that created you? That your wills and affections are changed; or that you have put on the new man which after God, is created in righteousness, and true holiness, Eph. 4. 24. Do you find, that notwithstanding of some remains of sin, which create you uneasy sensations, and make you often groan and travel in pain to be delivered, that yet the prevailing bent of your soul is indeed altered; and that your affections for ordinary, do run in another channel? That whereas formerly you favored the things of this World, now you savor the things of God? That whereas formerly you minded the things of the flesh, now you mind the things of the spirit, and have your conversion in Heaven? That you find a happiness in religion, infinitely sweeter and more solid than ever you found in any enjoyment of things temporal? Do you find, that whereas formerly you were proud, self seeking and somewhat revengeful, now you are of a more humble, soft, self-denying and forgiving temper.

Fifthly, with respect to your repentance; has it been sincere? Can you say, that upon the best enquiry you can make, that it has extended upon all sin? Is there no sin that you are yet habitually and allowedly indulging yourself in? Have you cut off the right hand and plucked out the right eye? Has your repentance extended to heart-sins; to that woeful principle of actual transgressions, which is original sin, which is daily, budding and blossoming, to bring forth fruit unto death? How do your former sins appear when you look back upon them? Can you reflect upon them with pleasure; or is it with shame and self-detestation? Have you left off the practice of sin merely from a slavish fear of Hell? Or, is it because sin is not delightful to you formerly, but appears a soul and hateful thing, contrary to your new nature, and divine life? And if by any sin you are conscious, that you have wronged your neighbor in his estate, or name, have you not only left off that sin; but as far as you were capable, have you made restitution to the party injured?

Sixthly, with respect to your duties; do you know what it is to meet with God, and to have communion with him in duty? Do you really know what it is to taste that the Lord is good; and to find him whom your soul loveth? Do you experimentally know what it is to get near to God; to come even to his seat? Do you find that at sometimes your heart seems to be fixed and your frame to be spiritual; insomuch that you have been even ready to say with Peter, Lord it is good for me to be here? Or with Jacob, this is none other than the house of God, and this is the gate of Heaven? Do the most solemn duties seem tasteless to you, when you find nothing of God in them? Can you say, that your deadness, unbelief and heart-wanderings in duty, are matter of great grief and vexation to you? Are you sure, that you don't rest or lean upon your duties, by thinking that God will be pleased with you and reward you for your duties; and by this means put them in the place of Christ? Do you make as much conscience of secret prayer, self-examination and medication, as you do of those that are more public?

Seventhly, with respect to your conversation in the World? Do you endeavor, what in you lies, that this may be exemplary? Do you in your dealings with your fellow creatures; steadily adhere to our savior's rule of equity, Matthew 7. 12? Do you endeavor not only to live inoffensively, but profitably to your fellow-creatures; striving industriously to do what good you can to their souls and bodies? Do you find that you have got the victory over corrupt nature so far, that you can render good for evil; can pity, pray for, and do good to those that despitefully use you and treat you ill? Are you charitable to the poor; and especially to Christ's poor, as such? And do you bestow your charity cheerfully? Are your hearts blessing God, while your hands are stretched out to the poor, that he has put you in a capacity to relive Christ's distressed members? In sum, do you endeavor to walk with God; to shun all appearances of evil? Do you endeavor to keep a watch over your jestuous word and thought; to take heed to your ways, and to live soberly, righteously and Godly in the present World?

Pray consider these few, plain experimental queries with deliberation and impartiality. Try whether with a good conscience you can give a satisfactory answer to them; or at least to the greater part of them. If so is a solid evidence that you have begun to bring forth fruits meet for repentance, and to live a life of real holiness. But if you are utter strangers to these things; if those false grounds, mentioned under the first head, be all that you depend upon, then you are secure pharisaical formalists, your house is built upon the sand; and will therefore when the storm of the divine anger comes, it will sweep away your foundation, of course bring down the superstructure and bury you eternally in its ruins. O then judge yourselves that you may not be judged!

Inference first, from this doctrine we may be informed, that a person may be a formalist and hypocrite, and not know that he is so. It is a wrong description of a hypocrite to say, that he's one who endeavors to impose upon the World, while he himself is conscious of the fraud. It's true indeed, according to the etymology of the word, it signifies a deceiver; but in its sequent acceptation it signifies, one who is deceived himself. Of this sort of self-deluding creatures we have several times mentioned in the Holy Scriptures. Such were the foolish virgins, Matthew 25. They thought they were in a good state, and went boldly up even to the gates of Heaven, with a confident expectation of admission. The like instance you have in the Church of Lacdicea; she thought she was rich, and increased with goods, and stood in need of nothing; and yet was poor, and wretched, and miserable and blind and naked; like Ephraim, of whom it is said, that gray hairs were here and there upon him yet he knew it not. And of this sort also, were the confident Jews with whom the apostle expostulates, Roman 2. 17. They are said to rest in the law, and make their boast of God. Another instance you may see, Matthew 7. 22. Many will come unto me in that day and say, Lord have we not prophesied in thy name, &c. Here are persons who thought they had a strong plea, no less than miraculous gifts, and yet rejected. And thus it was with the conceited Pharisees in my text; who confidently promised them all the covenant blessings of faithful Abraham. And thus, alas! It is with many professors to this day, who are securely resting upon their outward privileges and duties, while they are utter strangers to heart-work or experimental Christianity! And we have much reason to fear, that as they live, so they die. Visit them upon a death-bed; ask them, how they expect it will be with them in the eternal state that they are now just stepping into. They will readily answer, that they hope it will be well with them; that God is a merciful God; and that their whole dependence is upon Christ for salvation. But alas! Poor deluded souls! They confer not that God is a just as well as a merciful God. They examine not, whether ever they have received Christ by a true justifying faith; whether they have need of him, whether Christ has been revealed to them by God the father, Gal. 1. 16. Thus they die full of presumptuous hopes of salvation. Though their bones are full of the sins of their youth, which shall lie down with them in the dust, Job 20. 11. Yet they fondly imagine all their sins are pardoned. They go to death as quietly and with as little concern as if they were going to sleep. Like sheep they are laid in the grave, or in Hell (for the original word signifies both) Psal 49. 14. The sheep go as peaceably to the shambles as they would to the pasture, because they consider not whither they are going. Thus it is said of such persons, Psal. 73. That they have no bands in their death; their strength is firm; they are not troubled as other men; neither are they plagued. O how dies many a poor creature shut his eyes with a seeming tranquility, and never open them 'till he opens them in Hell. Hell will be a mere surprise to many who never fear their misery till they come to feel it. Its true they were often told of their danger; but they could never believe that they were the persons meant; but thought that all that was said, was rather applicable to some other person. And if we ask the reason why they are so many self-deluding souls under the gospel, where they have such excellent means of illumination? We shall find one cause among others to be this, which is, that they will not deal faithfully with their own souls; they will not know the worst of their case; they are like a bankrupt who will not look into his books; they will not look into their own hearts; but keep at a distance from themselves. Particularly, God, we have reason to hope, would help them; but for want of that pains which others take, and which they themselves might take, God justly leaves them in the dark; and suffers them to run into eternal blackness or darkness.

Inference second, this doctrine informs us of the dreadful state of the openly profane part of mankind. May a person have the form, and yet be destitute of the power of religion? Then what will be the case of those who are so far from the power, that they have not even the form? May a person attend sermons and sacraments, keep up family prayer, and in a word, walk in all forms of Godliness, be free from gross out breakings; be just in his dealings; give a part of his substance for the relief of the necessitous; in sum, conduct himself so that he can say with that discreet scribe, with respect to the outward observance of the commandments, all these have I kept from my youth up. May a person, I say, go thus far, and yet be an utter stranger to experimental religion and the power of Godliness? Then what will become of you who are grossly immoral; who lie, and swear, and blaspheme God's blessed name; who break your jests upon the scripture and divide serious Godliness; you who are slanderers, backbiters, and busybodies in other men's matters; you who cheat and over reach in your dealings; who cruelly oppress and grind the faces of the poor; you who have little or no regard to God's holy Sabbath; you who indulge yourselves in rioting and drunkenness, chambering, and wantonness; you who but rarely attend public worship, and who don't worship God in your family? Poor infatuated creatures! Alas! How wretched is your state! Whatever specious colorable pretences others may have, certainly you have no cloak for your sin; you come short of those that come short of Heaven. It is therefore without all doubt that you are in the way to hell. While you go on thus, how can you possibly get your consciences quieted? Don't you believe that for all these things God will bring you into judgment? And do you think you are able to contend the matter with him? Will your heart endure, or your hands be made strong, when you appear before the awful bar of that august and terrible judge. O then! Will you be wife in time! Tremble to think where you are going; and endeavor to fly from the wrath to come. Break off your sins by righteousness: kiss the son least be angry. And for your encouragement consider, that Christ is able to save to the uttermost, all that come unto him on gospel terms though their sins are like scarlet and crimson. It is not the greatness of your sins, but your impenitent continuance in them, that will prove your damnation.

But then, inference three, this doctrine informs us, that the hypocritical formalist is generally the most self-confident person. The true believer is of a modest, humble, and self-dissident temper. He works out his own heart; he sees it to be deceitful above all things, and desperately wicked; so that he has a holy jealously of it, and keeps a watchful eye over it, that he be not thereby deceived. He loves plain-dealing, and to have his wounds searched to the bottom. He desires to hear the worst of his case; and to have all his danger laid open to his view. He has a great many remarkable turns in his life. His Christian course is a mixture of day and night, light and darkness, hope and fear, joy and sorrow, alternately succeeding each other. Sometimes he has halcyon days; times of great quietness and comforts. He gets his spiritual enemies under his feet; and it seems to him as if they should never be able to make such a formidable head against him as they have done. God, by his favor, makes his mountain to stand strong, Psal. 30. 7. But an on he hides his face, and then the poor soul is troubled; his evidences are obscured; the light of God's countenance is hidden by thick clouds, that over spread the horizon of his sensible comfort. His former experiences do yield him but little support. He finds nothing to prop his sainting soul but faith; and even this at some times seems exceedingly weak. But this is not the temper of the hypocritical formalist. He is full of vain confidence and carnal security. He trusts to his privileges, his knowledge, his moral and religious performances, his soundness in principle, &c. So that he has little or no fear about his eternal state. He is not troubled like other men; neither is he plagued: he is settled upon his lees; he's like the man who sleeps securely upon the top of a mast. His whole life is of a piece; he has no changes, Psal. 55. 19. He's a stranger to those vicissitudes that the Godly experience: he don't know what they mean, when he hears them talk of God's biding his face and again showing them the light of his countenance; when he hears them talk of a hard heart, a weak faith, or some other spiritual disease; he imagines that these things are owing to a distempered body; that they are only the effects of a troubled brain and heated imagination. So that he looks down upon them with an eye of proud disdain; and esteems them poor deluded, fanciful enthusiasm. So little doth he know how God reveals himself to his own, as he does not unto the world. May God, in mercy to their poor souls, humble the pride of these self-righteous Pharisees, and make them sensible of their wretchedness!

Inference four, are visible church members so apt to rely upon the form of religion, and to be so full of vain confidence; then hence we may see the necessity of preaching terror. Ministers, when they have such persons to deal with, (and alas! Where is the congregation that is free of them?) should be close and particular in their applications. They ought to endeavor to beat them out of all their false fortresses: knowing the terrors of the Lord, they are to persuade men; it is cruelty, under the false color of charity to do otherwise. O miserable physicians! Who skin over the wound, when it is corrupted at the bottom: who cry, peace, peace, where there is no peace? Who sew pillows for men to sleep upon: who content themselves with speaking a few general truths, without ever making a particular application? Such are men-pleasers, and so cannot be the servants of Christ, Gal. 1. 10. O! We had much need to have a care that our unfaithful conduct in this particular, don't render us chargeable with the blood of souls, Ezek. 33. 8. Ministers can't be too plain in their advices to such persons, provided they keep to their commission. What could be more plain than the words of the Baptist in the context; Oh generation of vipers, who hath warned you, &c. So in our text, think not to say, &c.

It's true, it may be said, that this is offensive to some persons: they don't love to have Hell-fire cast in their faces; and to be told that the axe of God's judgments is laid to their root.

I answer for this very reason ministers ought to preach terror, because these are the persons who need it. Their anger is his justification. Wicked men don't love to see their pictures drawn; but what then? It is a sufficient vindication of the abstract, that there are really such originals.

But then to conclude the whole, with a few words of
EXHORTATION.

Are there so many professors building upon the sand; trusting to lying words, saying, the temple of the Lord; and thinking to say within themselves, we have Abraham to our father? Then let this be a loud alarm to every one of us, to look narrowly into that foundation, upon which we are building our hopes of eternal life.

Is it not true the greatest part of professors are generally walking in the broad way; that many are called by the external call of the gospel, and but few effectually called; that there are but few that find the strait gate, that lies at the end of the narrow way; and would it not then be a rational enquiry for every one of us to say, Lord! Am I in the number of these few? What reason have I to believe, that I am building upon good ground, when so many are deceiving themselves?

My dear fellow professors; let us deal faithfully with ourselves; let us be willing to know the worst of our case; let us search with the greatest diligence; and let us beg that God would search us as with candles; that he would make the most accurate enquiry into our state. Let us cry out with the Psalmist Psal. 26. Examine me, and prove me; try my reins, and my heart. I doubt not but the Devil will take every way that lies in his power to keep you in your secure state; and one artifice which it is more than probable he may use with you, especially you who have been long professors of religion, is to make you scorn to call in question your state. He will be apt to speak in you after this manner, "Shall I, who have been so many years a professor of religion and a church member, who have been still accounted a Christian both by self and my neighbors, begin now to question my state? What if I discover myself to be in a bad state? A fine discovery indeed, to find out that I have been doing nothing but trifling and playing the hypocrite all my days; that I must throw away all my former labor for nothing, and build upon a new foundation!" I answer what if you should find it to be so? If you are really in a bad state is it not better to make the discovery now, than in Hell? Don't hearken then to the before mentioned suggestion. It is nothing else but cursed, proud corrupt nature, prompted by the Devil, that speaks thus in you. Examine yourselves therefore by the word of God; and in particular, by what has been said in the doctrinal part of this discourse, as far as you are convinced in your judgments of its agreeableness to the rule. And if upon examination you find, that you have been building upon a good foundation, it is well; I desire not to tease you with needless fears. But if, on the other hand, the character of the hypocritical formalists, drawn here, belongs to you; then I exhort you to go to work immediately. Down with your old building; dig deep, and lay your foundation upon a rock. Bring forth fruit meet for repentance and think not within yourselves, we have Abraham to our father; knowing that God is able of the stones to raise up children to Abraham. And that now also, the axe is laid to the root of the trees; and that every tree that bringeth forth not good fruit, is hewn down and cast into the fire.

FINIS.

The True Believer's All Secured:

A

SERMON

Preached at the

Presbyterian Meeting-House in BOSTON

March the 11th and 12th,

Being Sabbath-Evening and Monday after the Administration of the LORD'S SUPPER.

By David McGregore

BOSTON:

Printed and Sold by S. Kneeland and T. Green in Queen-Street 1747

The True Believer's All Secured

2 Tim. i. 12. later part.
I am persuaded that he is able to keep that which I have committed unto him against that day.

THAT person who has a precious treasure, if he act with suitable caution, will endeavor to have it well secured; especially if the times are perilous, and there be great danger of losing it. Such a wise precaution does the believer take. He is practically sensible that the times are perilous, that while in this wilderness he is in the midst of enemies, that all he has which is valuable is in eminent danger. And from this sense of things he is influenced to put his all into the hand of Christ. And as he is enabled by grace to make this wise deposition; so when he comes to reflect upon his own act, or consider what he has done, it yields him sweet complacency of mind, while he has a satisfying persuasion that he has committed his all into a safe hand, where neither the power nor policy of men nor devils can reach it, where moth and rust corrupt not, nor thieves break through and steal.

Beloved, here is a considerable number of communicants who have this day been at the Lord's table, among which it is to be hoped there are some believers. Some who have had faith in exercise, and who have been enabled to make a renewed dedication of themselves and all their concerns to a covenanted God in Christ. And so much as have been so happy as to do so, it may be a proper and seasonable exercise to take a back look upon what they have been doing. Such a reflection will yield them sweet complacency of soul; while they perceive that they have committed their all into a safe hand: one who cares for them and all their concerns with the most tender care, who is not only able but every way well qualified to keep what they have committed to him, as in my text.

In the preceding part of this chapter, after the apostle has given the useful salvation to Timothy, and withal expressed his affection for him, together with his charitable opinion of him as being a person truly gracious; he next proceeds to exhort him, which is the evangelist to the faithful and zealous discharge of the duties incumbent upon him in the exercise of that ministry which was committed to him. Particularly that he should be active and industrious in stirring up the gift that was in him. And that he should be willing through grace to suffer with patience whatever trials he had to meet with in the faithful discharge of his office. As a motive to excite him hereunto, the apostle puts him in mind of the holiness and excellency of the Christian calling and the gospel doctrine of which be, i. e. the apostle himself was a minister, and for which he suffered, as in the first clause of the 12th verse, for the which cause I also suffer these things, i. e. for the preaching and publishing of which gospel, and by this means endeavoring to instruct the poor blinded gentiles in the true way of salvation; I suffer, being wrongfully accused of the Jews as a seditious person, and by them delivered up as such an one to the Romans. For it is evident that when he wrote this epistle he was at Rome; whither he had gone in the prosecution of his appeal to Caesar, so that he was there in the quality of a prisoner. He adds, nevertheless I am not ashamed; which is of the gospel of Christ, of the cross of Christ, nor of this chain that I wear for the hope of Israel. Nay so far was he from being ashamed of these, that he counted them his greatest honor. Hence he says, God forbid that I should glory, save in the cross of Christ. If there was anything he would glory in, it would be this. He next adds the reason why he was not ashamed; I know when I have believed, or trusted, as the word may be rendered. Hereby is intimated that he had been enabled to commit his all to God through a mediator, and that he knew he had done so. It therefore imports not only faith but persuasion, or the assurance of faith.

But then comes that clause of the verse which I have more especially in view; I am persuaded that he is able to keep that which I have committed to him. The apostle here uses a very strong term; it shows that he had not the least doubt, nor indeed the smallest ground for any hesitation in the matter. Q. D. as God has committed to my charge the glorious gospel of his dear son, so I have again by faith committed both it and myself into his hand. I have committed the keeping of my soul to him as into the hand of a faithful creator. In a word, I have left all my concerns in his hand, both with respect to this and the future world; and I am fully satisfied that he is every way well qualified to keep that safe, so that herein I do confidently rest and am no ways anxious disquieted about the event of things. I know that infinite power, wisdom, holiness, goodness and truth are at the helm, and that therefore all will be well in the end.

The words thus introduced and explained do easily afford us this doctrinal truth.

DOCTRINE

That a person who knows what it is to trust in God, does confidently commit all his concerns into his keeping.

The doctrine is not only scripture truth, as may appear from innumerable texts; but it is a truth plain from this text, as may be easily seen. In the prosecution of it I would propose this following method;

First, enquire what is that which a believer by faith commits to a covenanted God in Christ.

Secondly, what assurance the person has, that the trust shall be kept safe, and that he shall have a good account of it in the end. And then make application.

1. I begin with the first of these in order; i. e. to enquire what it is that a believer by faith commits to Christ, or which is the same, to a covenanted God in Christ. To this I answer in general, that he commits to this keeper all his affairs, public and private, personal and relative, spiritual and secular, for time and eternity. In a word, all that he is, or has, or is any way concerned with. But to be somewhat more particular: I observe that the believer commits all his personal concerns to Christ. Now these may be divided into spiritual and temporal.

[1.] He commits to this keeper his spiritual, personal concerns. When the person first closed with Christ, he saw him in every respect so qualified, that he could freely commit his precious soul with all its concerns into the hand. Nay, had he had ten thousand souls, he would not have thought the trust too great to commit to such a keeper. Now he considers that he who is the author, behooves also to be the finisher of his faith; that it is he who begins a good work, that can carry it on to the day of the Lord Jesus; that it is the great husbandman who first sowed the precious seed of grace in the heart, who best knows what culture, what watering, what nourishment, what pruning, in a word, what care of every kind it needs in order to bring it to perfection. And hence he commits the keeping of his soul to him, that he would work all his works in him and for him; that he would gloriously accomplish what he has graciously begun; that he would never leave nor forsake him, 'till he perfects that which concerns him. To be a little more particular on this head;

(1.) He commits his soul to Christ for guidance or conduct. He is deeply sensible that he is of himself a poor blind ignorant creature; that he has a difficult way before him, a mazy intricate labyrinth to travel through; so that of himself he is ever liable to error, ready to deviate into some wrong path which tends towards the path of the destroyer. He does therefore from sense of things commit his soul to Christ for divine conduct. He pleads with the wonderful counselor, that he would guide with his eye. Begs of him who leads the blind in a way they know not, that he would order his steps in his way; that he would send forth his light and his truth and lead him in a plain path. In particular, that when at any time he is much strained about what course to take, and greatly in the dark with regard to duty; that he would send his Holy Spirit to teach him what he knows not, and guide him to all necessary truth; that duty may be opened up to him, and that he may have grace and wisdom to comply with what appears to be his duty.

(2.) He commits his soul to Christ for protection and defense. The believer is deeply sensible that there is a formidable confederacy of powerful enemies engaged against him; that the Devil is his enemy, an enemy who is exceedingly powerful, cunning, implacable in his hatred, indefatigable in his endeavors; in a word, one who has all those qualities which render him a formidable enemy; that the world is his enemy, that it abounds with evil company and with snares and temptations of various kinds; that secular objects are almost constantly soliciting his senses and stealing away his heart from God; so that on many accounts he has sad reason to cry frequently, wo is me that I am in Meshech, Psal. 120. 5. That he has not only the Devil and the world, but that he has likewise a number of inbred enemies which are in some respect the worst of all; that he carries about with him a proud, deceitful, covetous, revengeful, unbelieving, carnal heart; a heart utterly averse from good and wholly inclined to Evil; in sum, that he carries the beasts of prey within him, and that his worst foes are those of his own house; so that he has much ground to cry often, O wretched man that I am, &c. On the whole, the person finds that he wrestles, not with flesh and blood only, but with principalities and powers; that his enemies are so many and powerful that he is of himself no match for them. He therefore puts the feeble new creature under the protection of the king of kings: begging of him, who is a king mighty in battle, and who has all these enemies in his hand; that he would bridle their fury, countermine and battle their fraudulent designs, and turn their counsels into foolishness; that he would by his assisting grace enable him to handle the shield of faith, yea to take him the whole armor of God, and to acquit himself as a good soldier of Jesus Christ; so as that he may come off a complete victor in the end, yea be more that a conqueror through him that loved him.

(3.) He commits his soul to Christ for daily support and sustenance by new supplies of grace. He finds, that as the outward man cannot live without new supplies of food, neither can the inward; that as nature, so also grace stands in need of frequent recruits; that when he has been a considerable time without the bread and water of life, grace in the soul grows languid and feeble, that the whole head is sick and the whole heart is faint; that as long fasting destroys the appetite, so in this case, that when there has been a long suspension of divine influences, his soul, which was want to be like a watered garden, becomes like a parched dessert. In a word, he finds that he cannot live comfortably one day without renewed supplies from the fountain. Daily experience seals that scripture truth to him, Job 15. 5. Without me ye can do nothing. Hence he commits his soul to Christ for nourishment. He looks to him for spiritual, as an hungry child does to a parent for bodily food: prays that he who has given spiritual life, would graciously support it; that the showers of manna may not cease to fall about his tabernacle, 'till he come to eat of the old corn of the heavenly Canaan; that he who gives to all their food in due season, would minister such supplies of every needed grace, as that he may be thereby qualified for the duties and prepared for the events of the day as it comes; that he may renew his youth as the eagles; and that as his days are his strength may be.

In a word, the believer by faith commits his soul or his spiritual concerns to Christ, that he would direct and protect, nourish and support; that he would graciously dispense every needed grace, by which the divine life may be prevented in the soul; yea not only preserved, but increased with all the increase of God, 'till at length the new creature happily arrive at perfect maturity, and sanctification terminate in glorification. And I would add, that the person who is enabled by faith to commit all his spiritual concerns to Christ, has a firm persuasion that he will do all this for him; that how many so ever the difficulties are which lie in his way, none of them shall ruin him, but he shall in the end be more than a conqueror through him that loved him.

[2.] As the believer commits all his personal spiritual concerns to Christ, in the manner he commits all his personal temporal affairs to the same keeper. The person has a practical sense of divine providence. He sees that it is in God he lives and moves and has his being; that it is Christ who upholds all things by the word of his power, and by whom all things consist, Heb. 1. 3. Col. 1. 17. that this providence, which has a general care about the whole creation, causing the lilies to grow, and answering the cry of the young ravens, has a more especial and tender care about believers; that these are to him as the signet on the right hand, or the apple of his eye; that on the behalf of these his eyes run to and fro through the whole Earth, 2 Chron. 16. 9. and that he has graciously laid himself under a covenant obligation. These things the person has such a sense of, that he cheerfully commits all his temporal concerns to Christ. He looks by faith into the new covenant, and there he stands promises of every needed temporal good thing. Particularly there he finds promises of meat and drink, Isa. 33. 16. Bread shall be given and water shall be sure; Psal. 37. 3. Verily thou shalt be fed: promises of clothing, as Mar. 6. 30. If God so cloth the grass of the field which today is and tomorrow is cast into the oven, shall he not much more cloth you. Promises of sleep, as Ps. 127. 2. He gives his beloved sleep; Prov. 3. 24. Thou shalt lie down and thy sleep shall be sweet. Promises of protection, that he shall dwell in the secret place of the most high, and abide in the shadow of the almighty, Psal. 91. 1; that he shall be bid in the day of the Lord's anger, Zeph. 2. 3; that the divine attributes are so many safe chambers to fly to in the evil day, Isa. 26. 20; that there is a strong tower to which he may have recourse, whither the righteous run and are safe, Prov. 18. 10. that in the greatest apparent danger, he has safety; a thousand may fall at his side, and ten thousand at his right hand, but it shall not come high to him, Psal. 91. 7.

The person don't indeed understand these promises of protection, as if by them he might assure himself of a total exemption from outward trouble. On the contrary he knows, that believers as well as others may expect that in the world they shall have tribulation; that they are bastards and not sons whom the father chastneth not, and that he scourgeth every son whom he receiveth. In a word, that in this respect all things come alike to all, so that hereby we can't know good or evil, love and hatred. But his comfort is, that God has absolutely promised, that he will be with him in trouble and will deliver him, Psal. 91 15. has bid him, whatever is his burden, to cast it upon him, and he will sustain it, Psal. 55. 22. has said, when thou walketh through the waters I will be with thee, &c. Isa. 43. 2. and, I will never leave thee nor forsake thee, Heb. 13. 5.

In time, the believer finds in the new covenant, promises for every particular case: and what is still more, he has faith to take hold upon these promises. He beholds by the eye of faith the veracity of God bound for the fulfillment of every particular promise of the new covenant; which is therefore more firm in his esteem than a mountain of brass. He knows that this word of God is a tried word, Psal. 18. 30; and that none has ever found him worse than his word. So that he most cheerfully and heartily commits all his temporal affairs to God in Christ. And whatever befalls him in his temporal concerns, let it be worldly honor or disgrace, sickness or health, riches or poverty, many sorrows or much worldly ease and tranquility; he is enabled by grace to make it welcome: for this tells him, it is best for him; and he cries out, the lines are fallen to me in pleasant places, and I have a goodly heritage. If God would leave things at his option, and say, choose this or that; he would make no choice, but would leave it with a wise and sovereign God that he should choose for him.

But then I would observe farther, that as the believer commits all his personal concerns, whether spiritual or temporal into the hand of Christ; so he commits all his relative concerns into the same hand. Here a very large field would open itself, should I pretend to take notice of all the several stations and relations among mankind. I shall therefore mention only a few of the most important.

As for instance, does the person stand in the station of a magistrate, whether of a king as supreme, or in any of those subordinate places of trust in the commonwealth, whether legislative or executive, whether higher or lower; he will be careful to commit himself and this his office to a covenanted God in Christ. Begging of him by whom kings reign and princes decree justice, him who is the giver of every good and perfect gift; that he would graciously bestow upon him such a measure of wisdom, integrity, courage, zeal, patience, public spirit, and every other needed qualification, as may enable him to serve his generation, and in some good measure to answer the end of his vocation; that he may conduct himself as the minister of God for good, and may be a great blessing to the people among whom he officiates.

Or does he sustain the station of a military officer, he will be careful to commit himself and his office to the same keeper; looking to the God of the armies of Israel, for the needed qualifications. Is he called forth to action against the enemies of the commonwealth? He desires to go forth against them in the strength of the Lord God; he would fight under the banner of the lion of the tribe of Judah, who well deserves the name of a king mighty in battle. As he doth not think it beneath a soldier to commit himself to God by prayer, begging that his head may be covered in the day of battle, and that his endeavors may be crowned with victory and success; so he is solicitous to have the prayers of God's people engaged for him. He believes firmly that though the horse be prepared for battle, yet safety is from the Lord; that therefore if God's people are enabled to pray servently, he is the more likely to have success; that if Moses hold up his hand Israel shall prevail.

Or does he sustain the sacred office of a minister of the gospel, has he the glorious gospel of the dear redeemer committed to his trust, as 1 Tim. 6. 20. which is indeed one of the weightiest trusts that a poor mortal can be charged with; how careful will he be to commit himself and his vocation to a covenanted God. Confidently believing, that he who has accounted him faithful and put into the ministry, will give him a sufficiency of strength and grace for the right discharge of the great important and difficult duties pertaining to that office; that he who sends none on a warfare at his own charges, and who has expressly said, my grace is sufficient for thee, will enable him to feed the flock of God with the wholesome food of sound doctrine; to direct them by the footsteps of the flock in the paths of truth and holiness; watching for souls as one who expects to give an account; being instant in season and out of season, and traveling in birth 'till Christ be formed in them; teaching both publicly and from house to house repentance towards God and faith towards the Lord Jesus Christ. In a word, that he will enable him to do or suffer whatever he is called to in the faithful discharge of the ministry committed to him.

Or does he stand in the relation of the head of a family; he is careful to commit himself and family to a covenanted God in Christ. He feels the weight of souls committed to his care by the great father of the family of Heaven and Earth. Has the Lord blessed him with a number of dear children; how affectionately, how frequently does he commit them to God? He does so, not only at the time of their solemn dedication to God in baptism; but generally when ever he approaches the throne of grace in prayer, he desires nothing more than to lend them to the Lord forever, as Hannah did Samuel; and he is earnest that God would graciously accept of the dedication; that he would vouchsafe to be his God and the God of his seed; that the oil of grace which has been poured upon his head, may descend to the skirts of his garments; that the salvation which is come to him, may come to his holy household; that they might be all the objects of special grace and redeeming love. How affectionately does he address the throne of grace in the spirit of Abraham, that pious, tender father, for his son Ishmael, Gen. 17. 18. O that Ishmael might live before thee. How careful is he to have them early indoctrinated in the wholesome principles of Christian faith? What pains does he take to have their tender minds deeply impressed with a serious affecting sense of their lost estate by nature, and the absolute need of a savior? And though he sees no present desirable effect of his pious endeavors of this kind; yet he don't despair, but continues in a patient, industrious use of means, hoping that the Lord will in his own good time bless his endeavors by sealing their instruction. Does he see in them any hopeful buddings, though but the smallest sign of some good thing toward the Lord; how tenderly does he cherish the good beginnings, what care does he take that the smoking flax be not quenched, nor the bruised reed broke? Are they as yet in their green youth, but raw and unexperienced in the world; how faithfully and yet tenderly will he caution them of their danger? How earnest that they may have that divine conduct whereby they may be kept from the path of the destroyer; that they may have grace to fly youthful lusts, and to shun those vanities and follies to which their age does more immediately expose them? Are they or any of them situated at a distance from him, so that he has not the advantage of keeping them under his eye, especially if they are in such places and stations as renders them more liable to temptation? How often will he be committing them to the great keeper of Israel, who can preserve them from every snare? How does he, after the example of holy Job, make it his daily practice to offer up sacrifice for them, least peradventure they may have sinned and cursed God in their hearts.

But farther, the person stands in the relation of a member to the visible church, and he is a member to a covenanted God in Christ. As a man is apt to have a particular regard for his native country, the believer has for the church. And indeed no wonder;

all his well springs are in her. Here it was that the new man first drew breath. Psal. 87. 5 -7. This and that man was born in her. Here the believer has often gathered and eaten the heavenly manna. Here he has been made the happy recipient of those nourishing showers of divine influence which have made his soul like a watered garden to grow and increase with all the increase of God. It was in these mountains of Myrrh and hills of Frankincense, that he has met with a savior, and had many a sweet intercourse with the father and his son Jesus Christ. On these and such accounts he has a high value for the church: as indeed it is most reasonable he should. As he regards Christ as his father, both with respect to generation and education; so he respects the church as his mother, in each of these respects. And O with what warm emotions of filial duty and gratitude does he frequently commit her to a covenanted God in Christ? Thy kingdom come is a petition which he appears to understand well, and to make frequent use of. Especially, is the church in any remarkable danger; how affectionately will he be committing her in this case to the great keeper of Israel? Her danger nearly affects him: he is like a man who himself is and who has all his valuable effects on board of that ship which is tossed on the tempestuous waves of a dreadful storm, and every moment in danger of being founded, or else dashed to pieces on some latent rock. In this case his heart trembles for the ark of God: his all is embarked in this bottom; so that for Zion's sake he cannot hold his peace. He commits the church in these circumstances to him who with his omnipotent word can change the storm to a calm, and who has said, that the gates of Hell shall not prevail against her. He feels such a temper of mind, as disposes him to that exercise enjoined, Joel 2. 17. which is, weeping between the porch and the alter, and saying, spare thy people, O Lord, give not thine inheritance to reproach. Or is the church actually in some sore distress; is it the day of Jacob's trouble, a day of rebuke and blasphemy? In this case he is grieved at heart for the afflictions of Joseph. Yea the sadness of his heart (with good Nehem. 2. 2.) will be apt to show it self in his countenance: he bangs his harp on the willows while he remembers Zion in distress. He commits the church in this case to God. Cries, help Lord! By whom shall Jacob arise? For he is small! Perhaps he tells the Lord, that he has said, I am with you always to the end of the world. In a word, he will endeavor to wrestle with God, and to give him no rest, till he return and smile upon his inheritance, and make Zion a praise in the Earth.

Once more, the believer stands related to the commonwealth as a member, and he is careful to commit it likewise to the same gracious keeper. The person knows that he is like to be very nearly affected, either with the prosperity or adversity that befalls the common wealth; seeing that which affects the body politic, must of consequence affect individuals, of which the said body is constituted. When therefore the state is threatened with some impending national judgment, or actually groaning under some sore calamity; as for instance, war, famine, pestilence, or any other sweeping distemper; in this case the person is deeply concerned under the hand of God. He is very apt to have such a sensation as that of the Psalmist, Psal. 119. 120. My heart trembleth before thee, and I am afraid of thy righteous judgments. He knows from his experience, how it was with the prophet, Hab. 3. 16. My belly trembled, my lips quivered at the voice, rottenness entered into my bones! Or the prophet Isai. 21. 3, 4. where he says, my loins are filled with pain, pangs have taken hold upon me, as the pangs of a woman that traveleth &c. And in this case he is careful to commit the distressed common wealth to him , who upholds all things by the word of his power, by whom kings reign, and princes decree justice: pleading that the black impending cloud may blow over, and that the storm may be changed into fair weather, which otherwise is like to lay the whole common wealth, and of course the church, under water; that he who would have spared the cities of the plain of Sodom, wicked as they were, bad there been but ten righteous persons in them, would not make a full end, but in wrath would remember mercy; and that in the mean time, while the storm continues, he would take care of his won little flock of redeemed ones; that they may be bid in the day of his anger; that as he snatched Lot out of Sodom, he would graciously pluck them as brands out of the burning. And the person is made to entertain a comfortable hope that it shall be so, when he considers that the Lord is Jehovah that changes not; that his power is as great as ever, his hand is not shortened that he cannot save, Isai. 59. 1. his wisdom as perfect as ever, that he as well knows how to deliver the godly from temptation, as in any former period; that his compassion is as tender as ever. From these considerations he entertains a comfortable hope that to the upright light shall arise, though for the present he be in the darkness; that he will bind his children in his skirts; that they shall dwell in the secret place of the most high; so that the overflowing scourge shall not touch them, or if it touch yet it shall not hurt them, or if it hurt at present, yet that hurt shall terminate in their final happiness.

And thus I have, as I proposed, endeavored to show that the believer commit his all to Christ; all his affairs, personal and relative, spiritual and temporal. Now this is certainly a very great truth: he had need to be well assured of the qualifications of the person to whom he commits such a trust. Which leads to the second general head which is.

2. To enquire what assurance the person has, that the trust he has thus deposited shall be kept safe, and that he shall have a good account of it in the end; or against that day, as it is expressed in my text, which is that happy day when he has completely finished the time of his probation, is got beyond the reach of all danger, and has actually entered upon the Joy of his Lord. To this I answer, in the general, that the believer has all the assurance upon this head that he can reasonably desire: the person in whose hand he has lodged the precious treasure being every way qualified to keep safe the most important trust. I would show how excellently he is qualified to this end in a few particulars: and.

(1.) I would observe that he is omnipotent. The consideration of this perfection yields great encouragement to the believer to commit his all into the hand of Christ. If we acted with sufficient caution we would not commit a precious treasure into the hand of a weak person; especially if he is situated among rapacious enemies, who we knew were watching an opportunity to seize the said treasure; though we had never so good an option of the person's integrity and fidelity; because although we know that the person would not willingly betray his trust, yet we know not how soon he may be rifled or plundered. But there is no such objection lies against our committing our all to Christ. For he is the mighty God, Isai. 9. 6. The attribute of omnipotence, as well as every other divine perfection, belongs to him. In this respect he thinks it no robbery to be equal with God. The souls committed to his care are all kept by the power of God, 1 Pet. 1. 5. The united power of men and devils cannot pluck a redeemed soul out of his hand. Joh. 10. 28. I give unto them eternal life, neither shall any pluck them out of my hand. He mocks and derides the feeble attempts of men and devils; Psal. 2. 4. He that sitting in the heavens shall laugh &c. He can say of the whole body of the elect that precious given number, as Joh. 17. 12. Those that gavest me I have kept, and none of them is lost. How safe is that person and all his concerns, who has omnipotence for his guard? His place is the munition of rocks; his foundation is like Mount Zion, which at no time can be removed, but high, and abides in the shadow of the almighty. So that though a thousand fall at his side and ten thousand at his right hand, it shall not come nigh to him. No wonder that believers in the exercise of faith show such intrepid spirits in the midst of the greatest dangers. It is not strange that the Psalmist could express himself in that undaunted manner, Psal. 23. 4. Though I walk through the Valley of the Shadow of Death I will fear no evil; seeing he had ground to add what follows in the next clause, for thou art with me.

(2.) He is infinitely wise. We would not commit a precious treasure into the hands of a simpleton, whatever opinion we may entertain of his honesty; because such a one may easily circumvented and cheated. But neither can there be any objection here against our committing our all to Christ. He is wise in heart as well as mighty in strength: yea he is infinitely wise. All the treasures of wisdom and knowledge are bid in him, Col. 2. 3. He is wisdom in the abstract, wisdom itself: he alone could say as in Prov. 8. 14. Counsel is mine and sound wisdom, I am understanding. As therefore none can cope with his power, so none can cheat or outwit him. Here is certainly great encouragement to the believer to commit his all into his hand. O believer, are you sensible of your own folly, that your enemies are too subtle for you, that you are easily imposed upon by false appearances, that you are too apt to be led astray by such as lie in wait to deceive from the footsteps of the flock; then commit your self and your concerns to this wise Lord: he'll guide you by his counsel; he'll keep you from the path of the destroyer; he will lead you safe through all the intricate windings of this mazy dessert, 'till he brings you safe to the land of light and glory.

(3.) He is omniscient. A person may have great power and wisdom, and yet be in danger of surprise from a guileful cunning enemy. No humane, no finite understanding can foresee everything of this nature that may happen. So that to such a one there is still danger, at least a possibility of being taken at unawares. Some contingency may emerge, which while it was future could not be foreseen by the most fore-sighty finite understanding. But here can be no objection against our committing our all to Christ. For let it be considered, that he omnipresent so he is omniscient: he knows all things, Jer. 23. 24. Can any hide himself in secret place and not see him, saith the Lord. Do not I fill Heaven and Earth? Saith the Lord. His eye is like a flame of fire that penetrates into every latent corner. It cannot but be so: he that created the ear, must hear; he that formed the eye must see. He that teaches man knowledge, himself behooves to know, Psal. 94. 9, 10. All the deep plots of his enemies are perfectly transparent to him. He is present at their bed chambers; yea knows their thoughts afar off. He perfectly sees through their whole scheme, though laid with never so much diabolical cunning: and when they go upon the execution of it, in order to which they manage with all possible security and craft, like moles working underground, fondly dreaming of success; he meets them with a countermine were they have got half way, blowing up all their hellish machinations, and turning their counsels into foolishness. Many such instances we have upon file in history sacred and profane. Beloved, though we know not what our enemies spiritual or temporal may be hatching against us; yet he to whom we have committed our all knows. Here is great encouragement.

(4.) I might add (but that it is included in the last particular) as he is omniscient, so he is vigilant. How sagacious and foresightly so ever a person may be; yet if we know him to be at some times seized with fits of indolency or carelessness, it would be dangerous to deposit a precious treasure into his hand. But here can be no danger in committing our all to Christ. For he has the most tender, constant, vigilant eye over his charge. His vineyard among other accommodations has a tower, which is a watch tower, in the midst of it, Isai. 5. 1, 2. least any hurt the most tender plant in it. He keeps it night and day, Isai. 27. 3. His eyes are ever upon it: his enemies come when they will, can never catch him asleep. Psal. 121. 4. Behold, he that keepeth Israel shall neither slumber nor sleep his eyes run to and fro through the whole Earth, to show himself strong on the behalf of those whose hearts are perfect towards him. 2 Chron. 16. 9. He knows his little flock all by name; and has as tender a care of each individual, as if he had but one to take care of. Here is likewise great encouragement.

(5.) He is faithful and true. Let a person have never so great abilities; yet had we just cause to suspect his fidelity, we should be afraid to trust him with a precious treasure. But in this respect a believer has not the least ground to fear when he commits his all to Christ. He is the faithful and true witness, the God that cannot lie. As it is simply impossible that he should be deceived, so it is equally impossible that he should impose upon others. Now this his faithfulness or veracity is plighted to his people in the new covenant. His word is gone forth; nay he has not only given his word, but his oath; Psal. 87. 35. Once have I sworn by my holiness. And to Abraham, because he could swear by no greater, he swear by himself, Heb. 6. 13. If any enquire what it is that he has promised, nay sworn, and to which his truth is bound for the performance? I answer more generally, that he'll guide them by his counsel; that he'll keep what they commit to him: that he will take care of them and all their concerns. Here a large field would open to expatiate upon; but that it would be too great to say, that there is no case a believer can possibly be in, but there is some promise of the new covenant adapted to it. To instance in a few particulars. Are they undertaking any great affair, and solicitous about the event; he has said, commit thy way to the Lord, trust in him, and he will bring it to pass, Psal. 37. 5. Are they under great fear from the prospect of some impending evil, whether national, domestic, or personal; he says, fear not, for I am with thee; be not dismayed, for I am thy God, Isai. 41. 10. Fear not thou worm Jacob, ver. 1. Are they under great spiritual darkness, their evidences being gone out of sight; he says, who is this that feareth the Lord, that obeyeth the voice of his servant, that walketh in darkness & hath no light; let him trust in the name of the Lord, and stay upon his God. Have they a dark scene before them, nothing but a sea of trouble to go through, which plainly appears inevitable; he says, when thou walketh through the waters I will be with thee, and the Rivers they shall not overflow thee, Isai. 43. 2. Are they actually in the midst of trouble; he says, I will be with him in trouble, Psal. 91. 15. Are they under any sorrowful bereavement; as for instance, are they the widow and fatherless; he is the widow's judge, her husband, and father to the fatherless; he says, leave thy fatherless children, and I will preserve them alive, and let thy widows trust in me. Are they strangers in a strange land; he is the strangers shield, Psal. 146. 9. Are they scoffed at, and ill treated for their steady adherence to his cause; he says, blessed are ye, when men shall revile you, and persecute you, and say all manner of evil against you falsely for my sake, Mat. 5. 11. Have they been guilty of any sin against redeeming love, are cut to the heart with a painful sense of it, would gladly return, but know not how to hold up their face in the presence of that God whom they have offended; he says, turn O backsliding children, for I am married unto you. Jer. 3. 14. Return ye backsliding children, and I will heal your backslidings, ver 22. Are they at a loss with what words to address an offended God upon their return; rather than this should be any stop, he will put the words in their mouth, Hos. 14. 2. Take with you words and return unto the Lord &c.

But I stop, because it would be next to endless to go through all particulars of this nature. Let it suffice then to say, that there is some particular promise adapted to ever case a believer may be in at anytime. Beloved, these do well deserve the name of exceeding great and precious promises, as 2 Pet. 1. 4. And however the infidel may scoff at the believer for his firm and confident trust in the promises; yet this trust is well grounded, the veracity of God is engaged for the fulfillment of each of them. Methinks here is great encouragement to put our all into the hand of Christ.

(6.) God has instructed Christ with greater affairs than any we have to commit to him. Here is great encouragement; because we are sure that infinite wisdom would not make an injudicious choice, by committing a precious treasure to an unqualified person. If it be enquired what are these grand concerns which are committed to this glorious person by God. I answer; creation, providence, redemption, and judgment, are all committed to him. (1) Creation. It was by him that he made the worlds, Heb. 1. 1. It was he who by his almighty that spoke the created Universe into being: He spoke and it was done; be commanded and it stood fast. See Joh. 1. 3. All things were made by him: and without him was not anything that was made. (2) Providence. He sits supreme in the providential kingdom; and with his omnipotent hand upholds the world which he hath made. Heb. 1. 3. He upholds all things by the world of his power. Col. 1. 17. By him all things consist. This is he who not only upholds but governs the world; and to that end is vested with supreme dominion. Hence he says, all power is given unto me in Heaven and Earth, Mat. 28. 18. God has put all things under his feet; and given him to be head over all things, Eph. 1. 22. And hence we have him represented with the government upon his shoulders, Isai. 9. 6. (3) Redemption. When the sin of the first Adam had brought destruction upon this lower world, which having been made for him, would its probable have perished with him, so that all things were to a speedy dissolution; this mighty ruin was laid on him, that he should seasonably step in and bear up the pillars thereof. He was instructed with the redemption of an elect world; a work which no angel in Heaven, nor all together were qualified for; that he should not only bring it about, bur in such a manner as that no one of the divine perfections might suffer, but that each having received its due, all might sweetly harmonize. Mercy and trust meeting together; righteousness and peace kissing each other, Psal. 85. 10. (4) Judging of the world; this likewise is committed to him. It is he who shall fit an incarnate God on the supreme tribunal, and hold an august court, from whence there will be no appeal; where he will hear the cases, examine the witnesses; and give forth the sentence; which will eternally decide the fate of angels and men. See act. 17. 31. Because he hath appointed a day in the which he will judge the world in righteousness by that man whom he hath ordained. Of this the prophet (Dan. 7. 9, 10.) had a very majestic and splendid representation. And hence you read, Joh. 5. 22. that the father judgeth no man, but hath committed all judgment to the son. Now are these grand affairs all committed to him; is this deposition made by one who is infinitely wise? Then certainly we may with all safety commit our souls to him, and instruct him with all our affairs spiritual and temporal.

IMPROVEMENT

Inference first. From this subject we may learn why believers commit their all to Christ. As for the matter of fact, i. e. that believers do commit their all to Christ, or trust him with all their concerns. This is evident from the practice of the apostle in my text, and from innumerable precepts in Holy Scripture; where they, who are believers, are commanded to do so; which through grace they are enabled to comply with; as I have endeavored to show at large in the prosecution of the first general head. And as believers, so they are the persons who commit their all to Christ. For indeed the unbeliever, let him pretend to what he will, cannot be brought to trust Christ for anything. He will indeed pretend to trust, when there is no trial: but when creature-enjoyments fail, or dangers threaten; he cannot be persuaded to trust in God. He thinks this is a hard dark saying: it is but cold comfort to tell an unbeliever of the truth and faithfulness of God in the everlasting covenant, and how excellently Christ is in ever respect qualified to keep safe the most important trust; after all, he will not be persuaded to commit his concerns to the faithful keeper.

And if we enquire the reason why the one so cheerfully and confidently put his all into the hand of Christ, which the other will by no means be persuaded to do; we shall find it is, because the one is acquainted with him, which the other is not. The unbeliever has no acquaintance with Christ: he is an utter stranger to the only true God, and Jesus Christ whom he has sent. What was said of Eli's sons is applicable to the unbeliever; he is a son of Belial, he knows not the Lord. He hears indeed a great many fine things spoken of Christ; as that he is omnipotent, infinitely wise, omniscient, and vigilant. In a word, that he is every way qualified to keep the most important trust; but these things are to him only hearsay. He has no experience of them, nor acquaintance with the person of whom they are spoken. But this is not the case with the believer. He has had his mind supernaturally enlightened in the knowledge of the dear redeemer. He has not only heard of him, but he has seen him by the eye of faith. He cannot discredit his almighty power; for he has already had experience of it in changing his heart. In a word, he has a satisfying personal knowledge of his being every way qualified to keep the most important trust committed to him. These things are not mere hearsay to him; but he speaks the thing he knows; and can say as the rest of the Samaritans to the woman, Joh. 4. 42. Now we believe, not because of thy word, for we have heard him ourselves, and know that this is indeed the Christ, the savior of the world. And when once a person comes to have such a knowledge of Christ as this is, he finds no difficulty in trusting him with his all. Had he ten thousand souls, he would make no scruple of committing them all into the hand of this keeper. It was because the apostle knew whom he had believed, that he committed his all to him; and that he was persuaded of his ability to keep that which he had committed to him. See Psal. 19. 10. They that know thy name will put their trust in thee. O professor, do you find that you cannot trust Christ with your all, see whether the reason hereof because you have no acquaintance with him, no personal knowledge of him. Get your minds enlightened in the knowledge of Christ by work of special grace; and then you'll find no difficulty to commit your all and then you'll find no difficulty to commit your all into his hand.

Inference 2. This may serve as ground of reproof to those who have committed their souls to Christ, and yet are apt to be disquieted and immoderately concerned about things of lesser moment. One would think that the conduct of real Christians would be such, that there would be no reason to complain of them in this regard; and therefore no reason to complain of them in this regard; and therefore no room for this reproof. And so it would, no doubt, were it not for their infirmity and the prevalency of unbelief. But alas, too much practical atheism, too strong remains of infidelity, are even in the hearts of good people. Hence if the lively vigorous actings of faith be suspended for a considerable time; God's children themselves are apt to be much teased with anxious perplexing cares about various things: especially if outward difficulties set in hard upon them at the same time.

But believers ought to beware of this sort of conduct; they should watch and strive and pray against it. Believers, in order to cure them of this infirmity, would do well to consider that hereby they dishonor God, and bring reproach upon religion. When the unbelieving world sees them vexed about trifles, as apt to sink and despond in the time of danger or calamity, and as anxious about the event of things as any; will they not be apt to think that their religion is only an empty name, and that all the fine things they say of their submission to divine sovereignty, and their having committed their all into the hand of Christ, are only a vain boast: so that hereby religion is dishonored, and the irreligious are hardened in their sinful ways.

Moreover, believers should consider the inconsistency of their conduct. O believer! You say you have such a full persuasion of Christ's being well qualified to keep the trust which is put into his hand safe; that you have committed your soul to him, trusted him with your eternal concerns. Well then, why will you not trust him with your lesser concerns also? You cannot think that these are too minute, too small for his notice; since he has told you that the very hairs of your head are all numbered. You have it may be a numerous growing family, and know not how to support them, having little or nothing wherewith to do it; or perhaps you have a great part of your worldly estate at sea, in the danger of shipwreck, or falling into the hand of the enemy; or possibly you have a husband, a brother, a son or some other near and dear relative, in the war, or some place at a distance from you, where he is exposed to imminent danger; or something else it may be troubles you, so that you can have no rest. Is this the case? Why need you perplex your selves about the event? Can't you leave these trifles, trifles I say comparatively speaking, where you have left your souls? Can't you trust him with a few odd shillings and pence, whom you have trusted with your whole real estate? Have you not sufficient ground to conclude that his fatherly wisdom and goodness are exercised about your secular concerns, even the smallest of them, as well as about your spiritual? Has he not bid you cast your burden (of whatever nature) upon the Lord, and he will sustain it, Psal. 55. 22. and cast all your care on him, for he careth for you, 1 Pet. 5. 7.

Inference 3. Hence we see the safe and excellent state of believers. They have by faith committed their all to Christ; and therefore whatsoever is essential to their happiness is out of the reach of men and devils. So that the true believer is prepared in the main for all the events that may happen. And when he is in the due exercise of divine grace, and by faith sees his soul in the hand of Christ; he enjoys a peaceful calm in the midst of the most terrible external storms. He sweetly experiences such texts, as Psal. 119. 165. Great peace have they that love thy law. Or Isai. 26. 3. Thou wilt keep him in perfect peace whose mind is stayed on thee, because he trusteth in thee. Does war, famine, or pestilence, or any other destructive evil, threaten the place where he lives; yet still he is safe. Is it best for him to be preserved from the calamities of war; then he shall be preserved; so that although a thousand fall at his side, and ten thousand at his right hand, it shall not come nigh to him, Psal. 91. 7. Or though he should be a sufferer, yet this suffering shall eventually terminate in his good. In the day of famine he shall be satisfied, Psal. 37. 19. If it is best for him he shall have bread for his bodily support, or he be a sufferer in this respect, yet he has that which makes up the want of it, which is bread to eat that the world knows not of. So that he can say as Hab. 3. 17. Although the fig tree shall not blossom, neither shall fruit be in the vines, the labor of the olive shall fail, and the field yield no meat, the flock shall be cut off from the fold, and there be no herd in the stalls; yet I will rejoice in the Lord, I will joy in the God of my salvation. In a word, should any of the calamities come with which a sinful world has been oft visited from the hand of a holy God, or should all come at the same time, so that a most dismal day; yet still he is safe. The Lord will take care to cover his head; he shall be hid in the day of God's anger; he has chambers to fly to, Isai. 26. 20. He has access to a strong tower, whether the righteous run and are safe, Prov. 19. 10. Nay should he live at the time of the general conflagration, see the tops of the mountains begin to smoke and anon to flame out, the heavens passing away with a great noise, and the elements melting with fervent heat; he has no reason to be dismayed at the awful scene. All that is essential to his happiness is out of the reach of those flames; and he, according to the promise of him who is truth itself, looks for a new Heaven and a new Earth wherein dwelleth righteousness, according to his promise who cannot lie, 2 Pet. 3. 13. O the safe and happy state of believers! O that all would be persuaded to fly to Christ, and to commit their all into his hand!

3. I would proceed to close the whole with some words of exhortation. In which I would address myself.

(I) To unbelievers. Alas, how deplorable is your condition! You cannot but be sensible that you have eternity before you; that you have precious souls which must quickly take their flight into the world of spirits, there to take up their everlasting abode, either in perfect happiness, or extreme misery. These are great and weighty truths which do most nearly concern you; and yet have you not a conscience which tells you that you have never acted like persons who believe these truths? You are outside Christians, and that is all. You have never seen the danger of an unconverted state, and what a fearful thing it is to fall into the hand of the living God. You have never had a right discovery of the guiltiness of your persons, or the depravity of your dark minds in the knowledge of Christ. All that you know of his being so well qualified in every respect to keep a Trust, is only by hearsay; so that you could never yet be persuaded to commit your souls into his hand, to trust him with all your concerns. Have you not a bosom-witness that joins with me in saying that this is your case, as I have represented it? And that you are taking little or no pains to have it otherwise: so that your all is in the most wretched uncertainty, and liable every moment to be utterly lost without remedy. Alas! What a sad infatuation are you under! How foolish is your conduct! Yea how inconsistent are you with your selves! You would not act in your worldly affairs as you do in your spiritual. If your temporal estate be in danger, you will not rest 'till you have it secured in the best manner that is practicable. If your title to any part is precarious, you'll use diligence to have it ascertained. If you have a sum of money to lend, you'll not part with it but upon good security. If you have a ship and valuable cargo putting to sea, you'll not neglect to have them ensured; especially if it bee a time of uncommon danger. And yet you can supinely sit still in soul affairs, and satisfy yourselves with maybe's mere uncertainties! You say, you hope God will have mercy on you at last; but can give no solid reason of your hope. Is not this to be wise about trifles, and in the mean time to trifle in the most important concern? O Sirs! Consider how little it will profit you, though you gained the whole world, if you lose your own souls. Look to the Lord; that he would enable you to give these things their due weight.

(II) A word to believers. You have had such a sense of your indigency, your guilt, and misery, and of the absolute need of Christ and his admirable fitness in every respect for one in your circumstances; as that you have committed your all into his hand. You have instructed him with all your personal concerns secular and spiritual, and likewise with all your relative concerns of whatever nature. And some of you have been lately making a renewed personal dedication of your all to him in the holy sacrament of the Lord's Supper. Happy souls! You have been enabled to make the wisest choice, and all that is essential to your happiness is out of the reach of men and devils. I would only say (1) As you have committed all your concerns to Christ, be exhorted to leave them there. Don't be for taking them out of his hand again; as if you repented of what you had done in committing them to him, as though you could manage them better yourselves. Don't indulge a thought of this nature; which proceeds from unbelieving distrust, and is highly dishonorable to him (2) be frequently committing your all to him. Be often ratifying and renewing the dedication in the ordinances of his institution, both public and private. (3) Let it be your careful endeavor to maintain upon your spirit a deep sense of your utter inability to keep yourselves, or any of your concerns. This will have a happy tendency to excite you to be often committing yourselves and concerns to the great keeper of Israel. (4) Since you have so high an opinion of the qualifications of Christ, as to have committed your all into his hand; see that you endeavor to be submissive to the allotments of his providence, even in those dispensations of it that are most dark and gloomy, and hardest to bear. Remember, that those dispensations which are bitter in their operation, are often in their effects: that you are but an ill judge of what is best for you: that he from whose hand the dispensation comes, is the fittest judge; and that he has said, all things shall work together for your good. Let these considerations excite you to take all in good part from his hand. (5) If you would desire to leave yourselves and all your concerns more entirely in his hand, labor after a higher acquaintance with him. As it is thy that know his name that will put their trust in him; so they that know most of him, will be most apt to trust him with their all. Endeavor through grace to observe these and such directions. Thus, commit your way to God, trust to him, and he will bring it to pass: he will guide you by his counsel, and be your safeguard and pilot through the whole of your wilderness journey. And when you are come to the end of it, he will carry you safe through the valley and the shadow of death; so that you shall be able quietly to resign your breath, with, father! Into thy hands I commit my spirit!

FINIS

The Christian Soldier.

A
SERMON
Preached at Newbury.

AT THE
ORDINATION of the Reverend

Mr. Alexander Boyd;
To the Pastoral Office at New Castle, in the Province of the Massachusetts-Bay, September 14th, 1754

By the Reverend
Mr. DAVID MACGREGORE
Of Londonderry.

Rev. ii. 10. Fear none of those Things which thow shalt suffer. 2 tim. iv. 7, 8. I have sought the good Fight, I have finished my course, I have kept the faith. Henceforth there is laid up for me a crown of righteousness, which the Lord the righteous judge shall give me at that day. And not to me only, but unto them also that love his appearing.

BOSTON:
Printed by B. Edes and J. Gill, at the New-Printing-Office In King-Street, for S. Kneeland in Queen-Street. 1755.

The Christian Soldier

AN
Ordination SERMON

2 Tim. ii. 3.
Thou therefore endure Hardness, as a good Soldier of Jesus Christ.

CONSIDERING the vast importance of the ministerial office, and what are likely to be the happy or unhappy consequences of faithful or unfaithful discharge of it; there is great need that every argument be used, that may most powerfully excite to ministerial faithfulness.

And, as on the one hand, a just view of the glorious reward, consequent upon a right discharge of the duties of that important office, will, (its likely) prove an animating motive to ministerial faithfulness; so on the other hand, to consider aright the many and great difficulties which attend the faithful exercise of this office, may have the like tendency.

Such a view seasonably taken at the entry of the sacred office, may prevent ministers from repenting of their undertaking, or from looking back after having put their hands on the plow.

A right view of these difficulties, and counting the cost before hand, may prevent the unhappy fate of the foolish man, who began to build, but was not able to finish. This, by the divine blessing, may quicken ministers to apply to their work with vigor and resolution; may excite them to put on the whole armor of God, and to take all due care to be well equipped for the important service they are to be engaged in. With a view therefore to promote these good effects, I propose by divine help, to introduce the present solemnity, by saying somewhat of the difficulties that attend the faithful discharge of the Gospel-Ministry; and to that end, have chosen the words now read, as the subject of discourse, where the Apostle says, Thou therefore endure hardness as a good Soldier of Jesus Christ.

This Text and context, contain an address of the Apostle Paul, to the Evangelist Timothy; in which, he gives him a number and variety of necessary and seasonable directions, with respect to his fulfilling the several parts of his important office; particularly the first verse, he applies to him in these words, Thou therefore my son, be strong in the Grace which is in Christ Jesus. Be strong: i. e. be stout and courageous, fear not any enemy, or opposition thou mayst meet with in the faithful execution of thine office. In the Grace which is in Christ Jesus; q. d. don't depend upon thy own strength; that all thy springs are in this blessed head of influence; and that without him thou canst do nothing. Then in the second verse, he gives the Evangelist direction concerning the important work of setting apart fit persons to the office of the Gospel Ministry. The things that thou hast heard of me before many witnesses: i. e. The doctrines of the gospel, and the office of the ministry, which have been by me committed to thy trust: the many witnesses before whom this was done, has respect to the numerous spectators who were present at the Evangelist's ordination. The same commit thou to faithful men: q. d. Take good care, not only how thou fulfillest thy own ministry, but also who thou introducest into ministry; that they into who's hands the sacred deposition is committed, be not only faithful, but not able. Labor to have all the evidence that the nature of the case will admit of, not only that they be persons who have an honest intention, but also that they are in some good measure qualified to speak as becomes the oracles of God, and to perform the other parts of that weighty trust.

Then in the text he proceeds to say, thou therefore endure hardness as a good soldier of Jesus Christ. Here's a duty exhorted to, and the manner in which it is done. The duty we have in that precept, endure hardness, or as it might be literally rendered from the original super-evil, which is the evil of affliction: q. d. Expect a number and variety of difficulties in the faithful exercise of thy ministry, and be ready to encounter them with Christian fortitude, and to bear them with equanimity and patience.

The manner in which the duty is to be done, we have in these words, as a good soldier of Jesus Christ. q. d. to excite thee to endure hardness with the more patience, thou must remember that the life of a minister, is not a life of ease and pleasure; but on the contrary, a life of warfare, the life of a soldier; that ministers in the faithful exercise of their ministry, may rationally lay their account with the dangers, the fatigues and encounters of a long and hazardous campaign.

The subject being thus introduced and explained, in discoursing more largely upon it.

I shall first, point to some of those things that ministries may rationally lay their account to meet with, in the faithful exercise of their office; which will require their enduring hardness.

Secondly, I shall mention some of those qualifications which are mainly necessary, in order to their enduring hardness, or encountering the difficulties they may expect to meet. And then make application.

And according to the proposed method,

1. I am to point to several of those things, that it is likely ministers will meet with, in the exercise of their ministry, which will require their enduring hardness. For consider, that the visible church is militant; Christ's disciples while here in this world, are in

a state of war, and need to put on the whole armor of God, that they may fight the good fight of faith. The church in the present state is like a flock of sheep among wolves; she has her situation among lions dens, and the mountains of leopards. Believers, at present, are in a world that hates them, Job. 15. 19. They have many enemies, and these hate them with a cruel hatred, Psal. 25. 19. This enmity began to break out very early in the murder of righteous Abel, by his own brother: and wherefore slew he him? The apostle tells us, 1 Jeb. 3. 12. Because his own works were evil, and his brother's righteous. And it has been manifesting itself in every age since these words of God were pronounced. Gen. 3. 15. I will put enmity between thee and woman, and between thy seed and for her seed: in so much, that in every age, there has been occasion for the apostle's observation. Gal. 4. 29. But as then he that was born after the flesh, persecuted him that was born after the spirit, even so it is now.

Our Lord tells his disciples, that in the world they shall have tribulation; and that through much tribulation they may expect to enter into the kingdom of God. And what he told them, they have they have found true. Hence it is observable, that the world has proven an unkind step-dame to our Lord himself, and to many of his dearest followers. The Psalmist was not the only saint who has had reason to complain, as Psal. 120. 5. Woe is me that I am Mesech, and that I dwell in the tents of Kedar; or to say as Psal. 57. 4. My soul is among fierce lions, and I dwell with them that are set on fire. Believers in the present state have not only men, but devils to oppose them; they have to encounter all the legions of hell, with Satan at their head; they wrestle not against flesh and blood only, but also against principalities and powers, against the rulers of the darkest of this world, against spiritual wickedness in high places. Eph. 6. 12.

And as the present state of the church is militant, so ministers are officers in this war, under Christ the captain of salvation. It is their business to animate and direct Christ's soldiers to lead them out to action; and while they are doing so, not to shrink back themselves in the forefront of the hottest battle, and to make resolute stand against the united powers of Earth and Hell.

And as in the heat of battle, we see that the enemy do endeavor principally to say their adversary's officers, so it is not to be doubted but that the Devil and his party will bend their chief force against the officers in Christ's army. What our Lord says to Peter, is applicable in a peculiar sense to every faithful minister, Luk. 22. 31. Simon, Simon, behold Satan hath desired to have you, that he may sift you as wheat. He who was bold enough to attack the captain of our salvation, in the manner we read of, Matt. 4. 1-11, will no doubt, as far as he is permitted, try every method with ministers, that he may either overpower them by force, or circumvent them by fraud.

From this general view of the case, you may easily see that ministers in the exercise of their office, will need to endure hardness. But I would be larger on this head, endeavoring to point to several of the particular things which will require their enduring hardness.

And first. The opposition, and the bitter scoffs they may expect to meet with, in their faithful laying down the scheme of salvation by Jesus Christ, will call for their enduring hardness.

It is true there is nothing in the scheme of salvation which deserves opposition, or which is by any means a fit object of ridicule. On the contrary, it is the most benevolent, and withal the wisest design. It is full of benevolence and breathes nothing but love and compassion to guilty polluted perishing creatures, in next subornation to the glory of God, according to Luk. 2. 14. Peace and pardon, and holiness, high honors and special favors, to the most unworthy rebels. In a word, considering the benevolence of the design, it might reasonably be expected that the gospel, instead of opposition, would meet with a universal welcome; that every house and every heart would be open to receive the savior. It is certainly a faithful saying and worthy of all acceptation, that Jesus Christ came into the world to save the chief of sinners, 1. Tim. 1.

15. And as it is a benevolent, so it is wise design; the devise of salvation by Jesus Christ, contains in it the brightest display of divine wisdom that ever the world was acquainted with; so far is it from having anything foolish or weak in it, anything that is a proper object of ridicule. Everything in the glorious plan of the new covenant, is so well ordered, as to be worthy of being of infinite perfection. Here's wisdom enough and enough, to employ the richest speculative human mind. Nay, the angels of Heaven, though not so nearly interested as men are, yet they admire the manifold wisdom of God herein manifested, and love to pry into it. 1 Pet. 1. 12. But then it is likewise true, that the glory and beauty of the new covenant way of redemption, and the excellent wisdom therein displayed, are not discerned by carnal eyes. With respect to them, it is called hidden wisdom, the wisdom of God in a mystery, which none of the princes of this world knew. 1 Cor. 2. 7. Hence the apostle had occasion to say as he does, 1 Cor. 1. 23. We preach Christ crucified, to the Jews a stumbling block, and to the Greeks foolishness. He who said so, although perhaps one of the best preachers that ever opened a mouth, was yet counted a babbler, when he preached Jesus, and the resurrection from the dead.

And as the minds of men are naturally the same now that they were seventeen hundred years ago, so the gospel is apt to meet with the same treatment; and this not only from Jews, Mohometans and heathens, but also from professed Christians. Natural men, however they may be born and brought up under a Christian dispensation, yet they cannot see into several of the important doctrines of Christianity. As for instance, they can't see into the Doctrines of absolute decrees, or original sin. How an absolute predetermination is consistent with human liberty. How it is just or possible that by the disobedience of one many should be made sinners. Or that by the offence of one judgment should come on all to condemnation. How it is confident either with infinite wisdom or justice, that a sinner should be justified by imputed righteousness; or that the just should suffer for the unjust, that he might bring sinners of God. They can't see into the doctrine of regeneration, as importing the supernatural production and instantaneous implantation of a new living principle of action in the soul, operating so powerfully as to produce and immediate change in all the faculties.

These and other peculiar doctrines of our holy religion, are foolishness to them, and the objects of their hearty aversion. And therefore he who will preach them up, with faithful boldness, and apply them with closeness, may expect the trial, at least, of cruel mocking; and very probably will meet with such opposition and contradiction, as will demand all the Christian fortitude he is master of, to bear up under them.

2. The close and painful application they should give to their private studies, will require their enduring hardness. There is a number and variety of acquirements, needful to qualify for the work of gospel ministry, which cannot be attained, without close application to study. It were to be wished, (if practicable) that ministers of the gospel were versed in all the various parts of solid, useful learning. That they were expert in the name of universal scholars. But this, wished for, than expected; especially in a young country, where things are yet, as it were, in embryo, or in an infant state. But even in our present state, ministers should have some competency of human learning. As for instance, it is at least highly expedient, that the gospel minister understood so much of grammar and rhetoric, as to know somewhat of the congruity and elegance of language. That he have such an insight into logic and metaphysics, as that he be capable of making proper distinctions of knowing when an argument is, or is not conclusive; of reasoning with some pertinency and clearness of detecting sophisms, and of abstracting. That he did at least know so much of mathematics, as to render him capable of reading books of natural philosophy, with understanding. That he be well acquainted with moral philosophy, and with history, ancient and modern, civil and ecclesiastic; especially, it is needful that he be

acquainted with divinity, polemic and systematic, as well as practical.

Now these acquirements are not to be attained without study, yea, much study, which Solomon observes, is weariness of the flesh. Many a one has endured that hardness, by close application to study, that has brought on disease, and hastened death in the meridian of life.

But this is not all: as to the study he prosecutes in order to attain ministerial qualifications, will require his enduring hardness; so also will that, to which he behooves, to apply himself in the exercise of his office. A conscientious minister can't allow himself to put off people with a rude impremeditated extemporary effusion. On the contrary, he considers that the interest of souls is at stake; one of which is of more value than a world besides. That his preaching is about matters of infinite moment; that he is like to be the savior of life, or the most dreadful death, to them that hear him. And under the influence of such considerations, he dare not offer to the Lord what cost him nothing; but though it should be a weariness to the flesh, he gives himself to close study, that by this means he may bring beaten oil, to cause the lamps to burn. The foresight that this may soon wear out animal nature, and hasten temporal death, don't at all deter him; he had much rather it should be worked out in such employment, than in any other; and hence he gives himself to reading, to meditation and to doctrine; and deeply sensible that he can't prepare for the public service of the sanctuary by his own study, he's much in closet devotion, often pleading with the father of lights, that he would enable him to find out acceptable words, directing him to seasonable subjects, and the most profitable way of prosecuting them. In a word, he who will make conscience of private preparation for the public exercise of ministry will find need to endure hardness in this respect.

3. Faithful reproof is another part of his work, in the exercise of which the gospel minister will need to endure hardness, and has occasion for much holy courage. Reproving and rebuking are

parts of the ministerial office, as well as exhorting, 2 Tim. 4. 2. He must cry aloud, and not spare, lifting up his voice like a trumpet in showing God's people their transgressions, and the house of Jacob their sins, Isai. 58. 1. Yea, if there be occasion for it, he must rebuke sharply, Tit. 1. 13. Yea, he must not only reprove publicly from the pulpit, but when there is occasion for it, he is to practice private personal rebuke. The faithful minister must not allow himself to respect persons, or to give flattering titles to men; but must faithfully reprove the vices of the great, as well as the small. Though the person that needs the reproof be one in great power; one who has the estate, or even the life of the reprover at his disposal, yet this must not hinder him from a faithful discharge of his duty. The Baptist is herein a shining pattern; he was no stranger to the tyrannical disposition of Herod. It is not unlike that he was sensible and that he ran the risk of losing his head; and yet all this doesn't deter him from reproving the tyrant, on account of his abdominal incestuous marriage. Ministers must follow such an example as this at their peril; they must put their secular interests and even their lives in their hand, leaving the consequence to God. They must sometimes minister those reproofs which perhaps will be galling to the consciences of wicked men, though they should like the murderers of Stephen, be cut to the heart, or angry even to madness. It's true; the faithful minister is to take care that his reproofs be wisely dispensed, with respect to time, place, manner and other circumstances. He is also careful to avoid bitterness, to shun the spirit even of Moses, when he said, "Hear now ye rebels, must we bring you water out of this rock?" In a word, he should endeavor to apply these caustics, with all that tenderness that the nature of the operation will admit of. But on the other hand, he had need to take care, least under color of prudence or tenderness, he should be unfaithful.

This is another branch of the sacred office, in which the gospel minister will have much need to endure hardness. He will be apt sometimes (it is likely) to have the mortification of finding, that although the reproof has been administered with all possible wisdom and tenderness; yet by his faithfulness, he has lost the good will of the reproved, who has become his enemy for telling him the truth, and ever after bears him a grudge, and is ready to do him a mischief.

4. The gospel minister needs to endure hardness, in opposing errors and errorists. The apostle tells us, 1 Cor. 11. 19. That there must be heresies that they that are approved may be made manifest. Sometimes we see the sovereign and all wise God, whose ways are past finding out, does for some end worthy of himself, see fit to permit false teachers to enter into his church; persons who make it their business to corrupt the word of God, and who are industrious to draw away disciples after them. It may be, the errors they promote, though of a very dangerous nature, eating like a canker, and threatening the vitals of Christianity; yet are so speciously gilded, that the poison is not easily discerned; fair pretences are made of zeal for God; and such guileful methods used, that with good words and fair speeches, the simple are in great danger of being deceived.

In such a state of things, that minister who would expect to be owned as a good soldier of Jesus, must exert himself; he must not see grievous wolves entering in, not sparing the flock, or the little foxes spoiling the tender vine. And in the meantime stand by as an unconcerned spectator; but when he sees men arising, and hears them speaking perverse things, to draw away disciples, he should consider himself as set for the defense of the gospel, and not fly, leaving Christ's sheep in the power of wolves; but to contend earnestly for the faith once delivered to the saints, endeavoring with all learning and sound Doctrine, to convince the gainsayers; using his best skill to establish the flock in the laboring truths of the day, and to reduce any that are wavering, and begin to be drawn aside from their steadfastness.

5. Ministers need to endure hardness, in that careful watch they are to keep over the flock. Christ's flock have much need of a careful watch over them, considering what foolish sheep they are, how apt to go astray, and what vigilant, subtle enemies are

engaged against them. And hence, although their chief safety is owing to the omniscient eye of him that slumbers not, nor sleeps, which is constantly exercised about them, without which, the watchman would watch in vain; yet it has pleased the great keeper of Israel, to appoint his ministers in the station of watchmen, Ezek. 3. 17. Son of man, I have made thee a watchman to the house of Israel. So likewise, Isa. 62. 6. I have set watchmen on the walls, O Jerusalem, that shall never hold their peace, day or night; and in the exercise of this part of their office, they are to guard against drowsiness. That's a sad character which we have of watchmen of Israel, Isa. 56. 10. which is sleeping, lying down, loving to slumber. As the minister of Christ would be owned by his divine master at last, he should take care that this character be not applicable to him. And in order hereto, he should have his eyes where Solomon tells us the wise man's are, which is in his head; carefully observing the state of the church, what are the practices of her enemies against her. In a word, heedfully noticing what are the phenomena of the natural, the moral, and the religious world; so as to be always qualified to give a right answer to that question, watchman, what of the night? Now is a work which will require great steadiness and application of mind. And those who will discharge it faithfully, will, (I believe) be often awake in a natural sense, when the flock in that sense are asleep.

6. There is a great variety of labors belonging to the ministerial office, besides what we have already touched upon, which will require their enduring hardness. Preaching the gospel is a very laborious work, as might be easily seen, had we time to view the nature of it. To hold forth the love of God to sinners in it's origin and first Spring, which is free sovereign grace; to open up the nature of that redemption purchased by Christ; to show what a wise gracious, glorious device the new covenant way of salvation is what a glorious constellation of divine perfections do shine forth in it; how well ordered it is in all things; how worthy in every respect of it's divine author. To display aright the manner of the application of this precious redemption. To preach the terrors of

the law to awakened sinners; representing Hell naked before them, and destruction without a covering; showing them what a fearful thing it is to fall into the hands of the living God. To direct awakened enquiring souls the right way to Christ, Steering them safe by those fatal rocks, upon which many souls have been wrecked and finally lost. To preach so as to suit a great variety of cases among believers, seeding Christ's sheep, and seeding his lambs; giving milk to babes, and strong meat to them who have their senses exercised. To make a judicious choice of pertinent subjects, well adapted to the times that may lead not only to truth, but seasonable truth. To be instant in season, and out of season, not willingly losing any opportunity that presents of serving Christ and souls. To make due care not only as to the matter, but also as to the style and manner of delivering divine truth; with the preacher seeking to find out acceptable words, using all the arts of persuading and animating; and leaving no mean unessayed to convince the judgments, and gain the hearts of men. This is labor! This is work! And he who will follow it faithfully must endure hardness.

But this is not all: they who think the whole of a minister's work is confined to the pulpit, and his preparations for it, do greatly mistake the nature of it. How shall he know what to preach, except he know the state of the flock? And how can he know this sufficiently, without taking pains to know it? 'It is needful therefore that he spend some convenient part of this time, not only in occasional visits to the sick, and catechizing, examining the flock as to their advances in knowledge, and conferring freely with them about soul matters; stirring up the ignorant and careless, warning the unruly, comforting the feeble minded, supporting the weak; teaching not only publicly, but also from house to house, repentance towards God, and faith in our Lord Jesus Christ.

I might also have mentioned the exercise of the key of discipline, a part of the ministerial office, which is often attempted with great difficulty, and which requires much holy courage, impartiality and faithfulness, as well as wisdom. As likewise, the administering the seals of the covenant, which supposes an enquiry into the qualifications of the subjects of these seals. A work this, which some ministers I know find very weighty and difficult. In a word, he who will faithfully apply himself to the various labors of the ministerial office will be apt to find it a work of great and sore labor and fatigue.

 7. The gospel minister will need to endure hardness, in bearing up under sinking discouragements, which are apt to attend him in the exercise of his office. Some ministers have more of these than others; but I believe none are entirely exempt from them, and some feel these to be many and great. Sometimes they feel the weight of souls lying on their spirits, with an almost insupportable pressure; they feel a degree of the same catholic concern, which the apostle speaks of, 2 Cor. 11. 29. The general interest of Christianity lies near their hearts; and it may be, they have the affliction to see religion low, corrupting errors prevailing, practical godliness much decayed, and matter daily tending from bad to worse; so that the things that remain, are even ready to die. Upon such a melancholy view of things, the faithful minister cannot stand by as an unconcerned spectator. His seeing Zion in this condition, will cause him to bang his harp on the willow; his heart trembles for the ark of God; he cannot prevent a good deal of dejection of soul, and it may be, he feels scarce enough of faith in exercise, to breath out faintly such a petition as that, Amos 7. .2. O Lord God, forgive, I beseech thee: By whom shall Jacob arise? For he is small. Again sometimes his heart is ready to die within him, to see so little appearance of fruit following his ministerial labors; to think that there is a sad probability that he shall prove the savior of death unto death to some persons that are very dear to him; that he must appear before Christ's judgment seat, and bear witness against them, that they despised the grace of the gospel, and trampled under foot the great salvation. O! it is a cutting thought. Sometimes he is sorely exercised with fear that he hath already proved, or shall prove unfaithful, in the execution of some important branch of his office; that he shall not be able

to give any good account of the weighty trust committed to him; that such souls shall perish by his neglect; and that he shall neither save himself, nor them that hear him. Sometimes he has unreasonable and wicked men, men that have not faith, men of beast like dispositions, to deal with; sometimes all men seem to forsake him, and none to stand by him; and what is worse still, sometimes his master hides his face. In a word, his discouragements are innumerable, both from without, and within; so that on this account also, he has need to endure hardness, as a good soldier of Jesus Christ. And thus I have shown (as I proposed) some of the difficulties attending the exercise of the ministerial office, which will require enduring hardness.

I proceed next to the other general head; which is,

Secondly, to mention, and a little to insist on some of those qualifications which are mainly necessary, in order to the gospel ministers enduring hardness, as a good soldier of Jesus Christ.

And first. It is needful in order to his enduring hardness, that he be a man of faith. Without faith it is hardly to be supposed, that he will fight the good fight, and steadily adhere to his masters interest, in the midst of difficulties, so many and great. But if he have some good measure of this divine grace, it will have a happy efficacy in enabling him to face and surmount difficulties. Faith enables him to balance the things of time and eternity, so as to give each its proper weight; to put the sufferings of the present time in one scale, and the glory which is to be revealed in the other; and by this means, evidently to discover that the light afflictions of the present time, are but as it were for a moment, so not worthy to be compared with the glory that is to be revealed. Faith sometimes enables him to see his divine Lord standing by him, and to hear him addressing him in such words as once he did one of his faithful ministers, Act. 23. 11. Be of good cheer Paul. Faith sometimes opens up the eternal world before him, and gives him such a view as Stephen had, when he said "I see Heavens opened, and the son of man standing at the right hand of God" Act. 7. 56. By faith he hears the captain of his salvation saying, as

Rev. 3. 12. To him that overcometh, will I give to sit down with me on my throne; even as I also have overcome, and am set down with my father on his throne. In a word, faith so fortifies the soul, that he is at times carried in a manner quite above discouragement; so that on a prospect of the worst that can happen, he is able to adopt the language of the apostle, Act. 20. 22, 23, 24. And now I go bound in the spirit to Jerusalem, not knowing the things that shall befall me there: Save that the Holy Ghost witnesseth in every city, saying, that bonds and addictions abide me. But none of these things move me, neither count I my life dear unto my self, so that I might finish my course with joy, and ministry which I have received of the Lord Jesus.

Let those ministers who would endure hardness, as good soldiers of Jesus Christ, put on the whole armor of God; above all, let them take the shield of faith; let them who have faith, labor for an increase of that divine grace, let them often pray the disciples prayer, Lord increase our faith.

2. It is needful in order to his enduring hardness, that he have a hearty love to Christ and souls. Where this grace is waiting, the person will be apt to do his work grudgingly and as of necessity. Where love is wanting, there will scarcely be any motive strong enough to engage him to adhere closely to his master's cause, when his doing so is attended with peculiar danger and difficulty. He'll hardly be contented to expose his life, or even his estate, or his name, for Christ and his interest. On the contrary, his behavior will be apt to be like that, Joh. 10. 12, 13. The hireling fleeth, because he is a hireling, and careth not for the sheep. But where this sweet grace of love is, it has a constraining influence on the gospel minister; it ties him by the heart to the service of his glorious captain, so that he never thinks he can do too much or enough in his cause. Under the powerful influence of this grace, he can cheerfully risk his life, when his master's interest requires it, with him who said Act. 21. 13. "I am ready not only to be bound, but also to die for the name of the Lord Jesus". We see what a

powerful principle natural affection is in parents toward their children, with what pleasure (under the influence of it) they go through a world of fatigue and sufferings to provide for them; such a disposition do those ministers, who love the Lord Jesus Christ, feel towards the souls of their flocks. So that the expression of Paul, with respect to Timothy, is applicable to them, that they naturally care for their State, Phil. 2. 20. Naturally, i. e. As a parent under the influence of natural affection, cares for his children. A faithful minister, when love in in exercise, does really feel the bowels of a parent, and can say with respect to the flock of Christ, as the apostle does, Gal. 4. 19. My little children, of whom I travel in birth again, till Christ be formed in you.

3. They should be persons who have made some considerable advances in mortification. This likewise is a very needful qualification for a good soldier of Jesus Christ. If a minister have an inordinate love to his carnal ease, he'll hardly be willing to follow his master in a thorny path, or to engages with great difficulties in cause of Christ. When tribulation of persecution arises because of the word, by and by he'll be offended. If he love the world with a prevailing love, it will be apt to take him off the cause of Christ. See a sad instance, 2 Tim. 4. 10. Demas hath forsaken me, having loved this present world. Hence that of the apostle, 2 Tim. 2. 4. No man that warreth, intangleth himself with the affairs of this life, that he may please him who hath chosen him to be a soldier. If he be excessively fond of worldly honor and applause, he'll hardly be willing to be accounted a fool, to have his name cast out as evil, and to have all manner of evil spoken against him for Christ's sake. Hence that of our savior, Joh. 5. 44. How can ye believe, which receive honor from one another, and seek not the honor that cometh from God only.

He then who would behave himself as a good soldier of Jesus Christ, should be one who has made some progress in the difficult, but necessary duty of self denial; one who has learned to make poverty welcome, if it should fall to his lot; who knows how to be abased, as well as how to abound; one who can deny his appetites and passions, when they become importunate and overeager in their cravings; or as the apostle says, who keeps under his body, and brings it into subjection; one who contrary to that character, Joh. 12. 43. Loves the praise of God, more than the praise of men. In a word, the good soldier of Jesus Christ is one who has learned to follow his captain in honor and dishonor, through good and evil report; so that he thinks not strange of the fiery trial, but closely adheres to his divine Lord in times of the greatest danger and suffering.

4. Christian courage and steadiness of mind, is a qualification much needed in order to enduring hardness. I join these two because they are a-kin, and often where the one is, the other will be found also. For want of the grace of Christian courage, even faithful ministers are apt sometimes in the evil day to give way to sinking dejection of spirit. They faint in the day of adversity when things have a discouraging and threatening like appearance, they are ready to give all up for lost; they can scarcely think of anything but of leaving their public station, and flying into some hiding place, where they may have shelter from the impending storm. When courage is wanting, every difficulty is viewed on the darkest side. For instance, a minister sees little or no appearance of fruit following his labors. On the contrary, it seems as though sinners grew daily more secure and stupid; in this case, he is apt to look on his dealing with sinners as to no purpose, and perhaps is just on the point of resolving that he will make no more mention of the name of the Lord. Or it may be, he is situated as Lot was in Sodom, so that he sees gross sins of almost every kind abounding, and his righteous soul is vexed from day to day with their unlawful deeds. In this case is ready to say with Jer. 9. 2. O that I had in the wilderness a lodging place of wayfaring men, that I might leave my people and go from them, for they be all adulterers, an assembly of treacherous men, &c. Or perhaps he beholds evident tokens of divine anger; it seems as if the Lord were about to come forth against his people with a sword instead of a rod; that the cloud gathers black and dreadful, and the enemy is about to break in like a flood. In such a case, through defect of courage, he is

ready to think of nothing so much as of flying from the storm. But when Christian courage is in exercise, it will improve all these discouraging appearances, as so many arguments to dissuade from an inglorious retreat. Christian courage will by no means admit of flight in any of the cases above named.

Are sinners very secure and stupid, so that nothing that can be said appears to have any abiding impression on them? Says the good soldier who has this grace in act, "I'll never the less continue in the use of means with these stupid sinners, though at present they seem to be hammer hardened under the word; he with whom is the residue of the spirit, can send a divine influence, which will soon and effectually soften them; perhaps the captain of salvation, who is a king mighty in battle, may lend me a chosen shaft from his quiver, which will reach the joints and marrow, so as to rouse them that are at present sleeping on the sides of the pit, with a dreadful sound in their ears. But whatever the event may be, I'll (through grace) do my duty, whether these sinners will hear, or whether they will forbear. I have reason to think that the sovereign will of God concerning them will have effect by my ministry, and that I shall be a sweet savior of God in them that perish, as well as in them that are saved." Or is it a time when gross sins prevail to a high degree? Though such a sad scene should open as that, Hof. 4. 1, 2. When there is little or no truth, nor mercy, nor knowledge of God in the land; when by swearing and lying, and killing, and stealing, and committing adultery, they break out and blood toucheth blood. In this case says the courageous soldier, the more the torrent of wickedness prevails, the more need I have to stand firm in my station, endeavoring to stem the rapid stream. Or is it a time when things appear with a threatening aspect; when the Lord seems to have forsaken his people, and there are sad tokens of his anger; or when the enemies of Zion appear to be hatching some formidable plot; yea, though he should have reason to think that their chief aim is against his person. In either of these cases says the good soldier with Neh. 6. 11. Should such a man as I fly? Nay, rather let me look on all these threatening appearances as so many loud calls to keep my station; let me stand between the living and the dead, and do my utmost to appease incensed Heaven, and so avert impending judgments. Shall I fly for fear of the plots of enemies, and leave Christ's flock exposed? How then shall I look my glorious captain in the face? How shall I clear myself of that character he has given of an hireling who fleeth because he is a hireling, and careth not for the flock? Rather let me put my life in my hand, and venture my all in the service of my divine Lord; firmly believing that he will stand by me to himself. That he'll make a fenced brazen wall, against which, through mine enemy's fight, yet they shall never prevail.

5. The good soldier is one who is acquainted with his weapons. Being faithful in the knowledge, and expert in the use of the Christian armor, is a necessary qualification of such an one as would expect to endure hardness. That a soldier should know his weapons, everyone will grant. Nor is it enough that he be a good theorist in this knowledge, but his knowledge should be practical. He should be capable of handling his weapons; especially he should be dexterous at the use of his sword. Even so every Christian soldier (but especially the officers in Christ's camp) should be acquainted with the use of the sword of the spirit, which is the word of God; they should be able to adopt the experience of him who said, Psal. 119. 97. O how love I thy law; it is my study all the day. They should love not only to study it as a science, but to feed upon it. And while they receive it in the love of it, and derive nourishment and delight from it, to say as Psal. 119. 103. How sweet is thy word unto my tast, I find it sweeter than honey to my mouth. The good soldier of Jesus Christ should be so well acquainted with doctrines, the precepts, the promises and threatenings of God's word, as that he may have a ready recourse to it in every times of need; and know how to use this spiritual sword, either to defend himself and his flock, or offend the enemy, as need shall require. And if he has such a knowledge as this, of the sword of the spirit, he shall be enabled to stand in the evil day, able to master every difficulty, to

overcome every temptation. He shall be an over match for all the power of the enemy; he shall both do great things, and shall still prevail.

Having spoken the two general heads proposed in the doctrinal part; I pass on to the improvement.

Inference 1. May gospel ministers lay their account to endure hardness, or to meet with great difficulties in their work? Then it may be inferred, that persons should not be rash or hasty in running into the ministry; it would certainly be wise in them to count the cost, and to weigh maturely the difficulties, as well as the encouragements which attend the sacred station; to make a close enquiry about what are their views in engaging in this office? Whether they have sufficient ground to conclude, that therein they have a single eye? Whether they have those qualifications, by workmen that need not be ashamed? To think of our Lord's question to Peter and John, Matt. 20. 22. Can ye drink of the cup that I shall drink; and be baptized with the baptism that I am baptized with? And to examine what answer they are qualified to give.

Inference 2. Are the difficulties attending the ministerial office so many and great? Then people should take heed that they do not by any part of their conduct, render them greater. It would be cruel to add a load to a heavy burden. People may do this many ways; as when they appear disposed to watch for ministers halting, to expose their human frailties; representing every lesser infirmity in the blackest color, as though it were the grossest crime; when they expect that a minister should perform the whole of his vocational labors with the utmost exactness, and yet do not afford him a competent temporal support; like the cruel Egyptian taskmasters, who would allow no straw, and yet demand the full tale of brick; or when they won't endure sound doctrine and ministerial faithfulness, but count him an enemy who tells them the truth; but especially, when they give a deaf ear to the great command of God in the gospel, to believe on the name of his son Jesus Christ, and so leave ministers lamenting their want of success with heavy hearts, saying, who hath believed our report? And to whom is the iron of the Lord revealed? People would do well to consider that faithful ministers are the ministers of Christ; and that he'll resent the neglect, and practical contempt, or the ill treatment of any kind, that they meet with; that he who despised them, despiseth not only man but God. Beloved, ministers are engaged in difficult posts, and they much need your sympathy and prayers, and friendly assistance. If you knew how hardly bestead they often are, while without are fighting, and within are fears; you would surely pity them, and do all you could to lighten their burden.

Omitting other uses which the subject might afford, I proceed to the last, which is the use of exhortation. In which, I shall address myself (1.) to ministers (2.) to candidates for the ministry (3.) to the candidate now to be set apart.

And first to you, my reverend, fathers and brethren in the ministry; permit me to say, that God who has chosen us from among our brethren, to come near to him, and to minister in things sacred, has in so doing, highly honored us. We are engaged in a calling, which though mean and despicable in the eye of a carnal world, yet would be no disgrace, but an honor to angels, to be employed in. To be workers together with God in that building of mercy, the plan of which was projected in the depth of infinite wisdom, from the morning of eternity: to be employed in the quality of ambassadors, to negotiate between the king of kings, and immortal souls, about matters of the greatest moment: what higher honor! And as ours is a station of high honor, so of high trust and importance; the great head of the church has entrusted us with souls which are his choicest jewels, and on whom he set so high a value, as to shed his precious blood for them. He puts such confidence in us, as to employ us in the quality of officers, to head his soldiers in the war against Earth and Hell. Let us think of the honor, and be humble; and let us think of the trust, and be faithful. Let us remember that all is grace, that we have nothing but what we have received, that one main reason why we are thus highly honored is, that by that by our meanness God might take occasion the more illustriously to display the glory of his grace; that he has put his treasure in earthen vessels, that it might the more evidently appear, that the excellency of the power is of God, and not of man. Let us beware of any action which looks like betraying our trust; on the contrary, let us be faithful to God and souls; let us labor daily in the use of means, for an increase of faith, for more love to God and souls, more mortification and self denial, more Christian courage and steadfastness of mind, more skillfulness in the knowledge and expertness in the use of our spiritual weapons. In a word, more of all those qualifications whereby we shall be fitted to endure hardness, as a good soldier of Jesus Christ. And whatever ministerial qualifications it has pleased the giver of every good gift, and perfect, to bestow on us, let us not bury them in the Earth, nor hide them in the unprofitable napkin. On the contrary, let us stir up the gifts that are in us; being infant in season; not thinking much of our hard study or toil, or bodily fatigue and experience of spirits, if so be, that thereby we may do any service; not counting even our lives dear, so that we may finish our course with joy, and the ministry committed to us of the Lord Jesus. Let us remember that there will be time enough to rest in Heaven, and hence, let us be willing now to labor; and let us not only be willing to work our selves, but let us do what we can to encourage others in their work. Let all Christ's faithful ministers endeavor to strengthen one another's hands.

If the Soldiers, but especially the officers in Christ's army, begin to turn their swords against one another, they are like to be an easy prey to the common enemy. O that this were duly laid to heart! It would powerfully influence us to cultivate that strict unity, which (through the divine blessing) would greatly strengthen the common cause, which would render us fair as the Moon, clear as the Sun, terrible as an army with banners.

And to animate us to exert ourselves to the utmost in our master's cause; let us consider that our charge is weighty; our account will be solemn; and that the time when we must make it up, is approaching. Let us with the blessed apostle Peter, remember that we must shortly put off this our tabernacle. Some of us, (it's likely) have almost done; a few years, or it may be months, and the present scene with respect to us, will forever shut. O then, let us do speedily and with our might, whatever our hands find to do. Let us crowd in as much service as we can, in the few remaining days we have left. And to keep up our spirits under the coldness and ingratitude of the world, the contradiction and opposition of unreasonable men. All our unsuccessfulness in our own hearts. In a word, all the difficulties of the campaign; let us look forward by faith to that happy approaching day, when Christ who is our life shall appear, and we also shall appear with him in glory; when they that be wise shall shine as the brightness of the firmament, and they that turn many to righteousness, as the stars for ever and ever.

2. To candidates: I would say, my dear brethren, we who have been acting our part as officers in Christ' camp, must soon move off stage. These mouths that speak to you, must in a short time be stopped with the dust of death; and we have our eyes on you to succeed us. 'Tis you, and such as you, that must fill up our vacant places, in the camp of the saints. Blessed be God, for some agreeable prospect of a succession! Be exhorted, brethren, to labor for those qualifications by which you may be slated to endure hardness, as good soldiers of Jesus Christ: and in order hereto, give yourselves to reading, to close study, and to prayer; and let all your endeavors be used in subserviency to the promised aids of the divine spirit. Beware of a proud, self sufficient disposition. Remember that a scriptural bishop must not be a novice, left being lifted up with pride, he fall into the condemnation of the Devil. Don't esteem yourselves to be already well enough qualified for the great work of the gospel minister; but on the contrary, endeavor to maintain a low opinion of any attainments you have already arrived at; and forgotten the things that are behind, be pressing forward. Let it be your daily

labor, to add to the fund of knowledge, either by getting some new ideas, or those you have, better digested. And let the governing principle in all your endeavors, be love to God, and concern for his glory.

3. I'd address myself to the candidate now to be solemnly set apart to the work of the ministry.

Your are now, Sir, about to engage in a station of great importance, and great difficulty. You are to have the preaching of the everlasting gospel, and the administering the seal of the new covenant committed to your trust. Your are to have the keys of the Kingdom of Heaven put into your hand with authority ministerially to open and shut, in the name of him who openeth, and no man shutteth, and who shutteth, and no man openeth. You are about to take the charge of a number of immortal souls, each of which is of more value than a world; on this condition, that if any should perish by your neglect, it is to be required at your hand. I trust you have known these many years, what it is to be a soldier of Christ, which is a character that belongs to every Christian; and that you are not now to begin the war with the Devil, the flesh and the world. But that you are this day, in somewhat of a peculiar sense, taking up arms against Satan and his kingdom, which is as an officer in Christ's camp. And you may reasonably expect to have the power and policy of Earth and Hell engaged against you. You are engaging in the ministerial work, in an evil day, a day of trouble and of rebuke, and of blasphemy; a day when religion appears to be low, and enemies of Christ and his cause are apparently prevailing; when a spirit of conviction seems to be much withheld, and the waters of the sanctuary to have lost (in a great measure) their healing virtue; so that the ways of Zion mourn, and faithful ministers with heavy hearts complain, that they have labored in vain, and spent their strength for nought. A day, when many real Christians appear in a sad degree to have lost the likely affecting views of divine things; when a worldly spirit prevails, so that there's too much reason for the apostle's complaint, that all men mind their own things, and none the things that are Christ's. When instances of awful impenitency and hardness of a heart abound; when sinners sin with a high hand, make light of their danger, mocking at fear, and laughing at the shaking of God's spear. In a word, the charge is weighty, and the days are evil; and to undertake such a charge, at such a time, is enough to make a frail mortal tremble.

And I make no doubt, my brother, but your spirits are weighted with it, and have been so before this day; that you have been carefully counting the cost, and revolving the difficulties in your mind. I mention these difficulties not to discourage you, but on the contrary, to animate you to apply to your work with greater vigor and resolution. And for your encouragement, I shall propose a few animating considerations.

First, consider that it is a very difficult, yet it is withal, a very honorable work you are engaged in. In the time of the flourishing of the Roman commonwealth, it was thought a high honor of being enlisted this day, and this, in a place of some considerable distinction too, under the banner of him who is king of kings, and Lord of Lords; the prince of the kings of the Earth, who esteems of the monarchs of the Earth, as grasshoppers. The apostle Paul esteemed this honor, a high favor conferred on him, when he said, Eph. 3. 8. To me who am less then the least of all saints, is this grace given; that I should preach among the Gentiles, the unsearchable riches of Christ.

Secondly, consider that you are to have your master's presence with you in the whole of your ministerial work. It's true, the work is great and difficult, and you may apprehend your self weak and very unequal to it. But remember you have a strong Lord to depend upon; and that as the work you have to be employed in, is his work, on him therefore you may with a humble confidence depend, for all that assistance you have need of: for who goeth a warfare at any time at his own charges? He can give you the wisdom of the serpent, as well as the simplicity of the dove; whereby you shall be able to countermine and baffle the most insidious plots of the Devil and his instruments, though they should work like moles underground, and dig deep as Hell to accomplish their designs. He can furnish you with a brave, heroic, undaunted spirit; whereby you shall be enabled to set your face like a flint, and with a calm intrepid courage, to face the most formidable assaults of the enemy. He can make you a second brazen wall, against which, though your enemies should fight, yet they shall not be able to prevail. He can temper your zeal and courage with humility and prudence, and self denial. In a word, he can give you the Christian temper in all its lovely branches; so that you shall be able to contend for the faith of Christ, with the spirit of Christ. Did I say he can? I may add, he will, if you look on him by faith, or depend aright upon him; for he has said, my grace is sufficient for thee, 2 Cor. 12. 9. This promise belongs to every faithful minister to the end, as well as to him to whom it was first made.

Thirdly, consider that you be faithful to your colors, you are sure of the victory. What soldier would not fight with courage, who is sure of complete victory at last? But this is the case of the good soldier of Jesus Christ. It must be so, for he has omnipotence on his side; the captain of his salvation, is a king mighty in battle, he will tread his enemies in his anger, and trample them in his fury; their blood shall be on his garments, and he will stain his raiment.

The most formidable party they can possibly make, is but as briars and thorns, before devouring flames. If then he erect his banner in the name of Christ, he shall do valiantly; if he be strong in the grace which is in Christ Jesus, he shall both do great things, and shall still prevail.

Fourthly, consider that there is a glorious reward consequent upon ministerial faithfulness. It's true; I cannot propose any great earthly reward for your encouragement: on the contrary, many faithful ministers have been obliged to endure hardness, in this as well as in other respects, to content themselves with mean fare, and some have been pinched for want of pure necessaries. And although ministers should have a competency, God having ordained, that they who preach the gospel should live by the gospel; yet it would be unreasonable for them to expect to live in the pomp and splendor of temporal princes, seeing their Lord has told them, that his kingdom is not of this world. But consider, that although you have no great secular inducement, yet you have a reward of a higher nature than the crowns of princes, and the peculiar treasure of kings and provinces, which is a crown of glory that fadeth not away. Think my brother of that day which is approaching, when the chief shepherd shall appear and you shall appear with him in glory; when you shall have a number of saved, glorified souls, all shining in the beauties of holiness, like so many radiant gems to adorn your crown of glory. O think of that happy approaching day! When they that are wise shall shine as the brightness as the stars for ever and ever. Or though it should be your hard lot to labor all your days in vain, and spend your strength for nought, and never to be instrumental of turning any to righteousness, (which I cannot think your master will suffer to be the case); yet even in this case, remember that your judgment is with the Lord, and your work with God; and that your faithful endeavors will be well accepted.

Fifthly, consider that the more you do in your station, and the more hardness you are called to suffer in the cause of your glorious captain; it is likely the more you'll enjoy of his gracious spiritual presence. When the apostle Paul was called before Nero, no man stood with him, but all men forsook him; yet he tell us, that then the Lord stood by him, and strengthened him, so that he was delivered out of the mouth of the lion, 2 Tim. 4. 16, 17. It was when the apostle John was banished into the obscure remote isle of Patmos, for the word of God, and for the testimony which he held, that he was savored with those glorious visions and revelations, which you have on record in the last book of the New Testament. If your Lord call you to great trials, you shall have proportional incomes of grace; you shall be able to adopt the experience of the apostle, and his fellow soldiers, 2 Cor. 1. 5. As the sufferings of Christ abound in us , so our consolation also aboundeth by Christ. So that you'll be qualified from what you feel, to unriddle these paradoxes, 2 Cor. 6. 9, 10. As dying, and behold we live; as chastened, and not killed; as sorrowful, yet always rejoicing; as being nothing, and yet possessing all things.

These, Sir, are animating considerations: under the influence of them address your self to your work, with a cheerful courage and vigor. Take heed to your ministry, that you fulfill it. Take heed to yourself, and to your doctrine; for in doing this , you will both save yourself, and them that hear you.

I should next address myself to the people, who are about to receive the candidate for their minister, were they present. They had appointed some of their number to act in their name, on the solemn occasion; but it pleased that wise sovereign, who does everything for the best, to prevent their coming. However, although not personally present, we have their concurrence in the matter. Had they been here, I should have said to them; that after a sufficient time for trial, they had proceeded to give a call to this our brother; and that said call had been proceeded in with as much order as their situation and other circumstances would admit of: that we rejoice with them, in that after a series of events, in which they have been liable to a variety of difficulties, and in which many changes have passed over them; that a bountiful Lord is at length about to bestow on them a minister, who we believe has obtained help of God to be faithful; and who we trust will be enabled to endure hardness as a good soldier of Jesus Christ. That as they had been hearing that he is engaging in a difficult work, so we hope that they will not by any part of their conduct, witfully add to his difficulties. On the contrary, that they would yield him that limited subjection and obedience in the Lord, which they had solemnly promised in their call; regarding and obeying him as having the rule over them, and who watches for their souls as one who must give an account. That they would remember whose name he comes in, and whose message he is charged with; and would esteem him very highly in love for his master's sake, and for his work's sake; especially, that they would receive that Christ and salvation he offers to them, as they would not oblige him to appear as a swift witness against them at the great day of accompts. That they would be tender as to the exposing any frailties they may see in their minister; especially such things as they have reason to think are no more then indiscretions, proceeding from mere inadvertency, without any criminal intention; that they would kindly draw the veil of charity over such things. That they would wrestle with God in prayer on his behalf, that he may be in every respect an able and successful minister of the new testament. And finally, that as he ministers to them in spirituals, that they would do to their utmost, cheerfully and liberally to minister to him in temporals.

May the Lord make ministers and people mutual blessings to one another; that so the happy day may come, when both he that soweth, and they that reap, may rejoice together.

FINIS

The following is from Rev. David McGregor's segment of the papers entitled, The Business and End of the Ministerial Office Considered and Improved – 1765. These papers addressed a controversial address made by Rev. Abercrombie.

Address after the Right Hand of Fellowship. By Rev. David MacGregore

ET me now address myself to you our dear brother. You have, sir, taken on you a great charge. The office is honorable, is difficult, and the consequence of your conduct herein is like to be very interesting. I say the charge is weighty. You have taken on you, the care of a number of souls, on account of whom the Son of God was content to be made a curse! I need not inform you that if one of these perish through your neglect, we have it from the mouth of God, that its blood he will require at your hand: a consideration I think enough to make the best of us tremble!

And as the charge is weighty so it is honorable. To be a messenger, an ambassador to the children of men about matters of eternal moment would be no degrading, but an honor to the highest angel in Heaven; the apostle Paul appears deeply and justly affected with a sense of the honor and the favor conferred on him when he said, to me who am less than the least of all his saints is this grace given, that I should preach among the gentiles the unsearchable riches of Christ.

And as the charge is weighty and honorable, so it is difficult. In Jer. 20. 7. we find these words, O Lord thou hast deceived me and I was deceived; thou art stronger then I and hast prevailed. The meaning perhaps is q. d. Thou hast persuaded or allured me so hast led me forward into the prophetical office, without letting me know fully the difficulties which attend the faithful discharge of it, which had I known, I should scarce have ventured upon it. If men knew beforehand all the difficulties that attend the ministerial work there is but few would undertake it. I hint at these difficulties not to discourage you, but rather to animate you to put on resolution, that you may acquit you as a man in your office; and for your encouragement you are to consider, that though you have strong enemies to make head against, you have also a strong Lord to aid you; the weapons of your warfare are chosen from the armory of God, they are spiritual and mighty through God to the pulling down of strong holds; if you learn to manage them aright you'll prove and overmatch for all the power of the enemy, and nothing shall be able to hurt you.

I would add, as the office is weighty, is honorable, is difficult, so the consequence of your conduct in it is like to be very interesting; interesting to the flock of God and yourself. By your neglect precious souls may perish, eternally perish; by the blessing of God on your faithful endeavors you may both have yourself and them that hear you. And as it is interesting to the flock, so to yourself. You have engaged, far, in a work in which your faithful of unfaithful conduct will introduce high degrees of happiness or misery in the future world. O remember that they that be wise shall shine as the brightness of the firmament! That unfaithful ministers are like to have their portion with Judas and such execrable traitors. That is a terrible expression of Mr. Flavel, speaking of unfaithful ministers, he says, "Of all the creatures of God, the Devils themselves not excepted, such ministers serve the interest of Hell the most successfully." And if so, doubtless their reward will be answerable, for the judge is one that will render to every one according to his work. These, sir, are weighty animating considerations, under the influence of them be excited to apply yourself to your work in good earnest, resolve through grace, that however some others in the ministry may serve the Lord with greater gifts and superior talents, yet none shall serve him with a more hearty good will; don't be excessive afraid of wearing out to soon by hard labor, never think you can do much or enough for him who has counted you faithful, and put you into the ministry; not reckoning even your life dear if so be you might finish your course with joy, and the ministry committed to you by the Lord Jesus. Endeavor to inspire your people with right sentiments of Christianity, teach them not only to distinguish between truth and error, but between truth and truth, i. e. truths of greater and lesser importance; warn them of the danger of bigotry on the one hand and latitudinariasm, but on the other. Endeavor not only to promote reformation, but conversion among them; show them that except a man be born again he cannot see the kingdom of God. That except for their righteousness exceed the righteousness of the Scribes and Pharisees they can in no case enter into the kingdom of Heaven.

Christian UNITY and PEACE Recommended.

A

SERMON

PREACHED

At Rowley, May 9th, 1765

BY

DAVID MACGREGORE, A. M.

BOSTON

Printed by W. Mc ALPINE and J. FLEEMING in Marlborough-Street   M,DCC,LXV.

Christian UNITY and PEACE

2 Cor. xiii. II.

Finally brethren farewell: Be perfect, be of good comfort, be of one mind, live in peace; and the God of love and peace shall be with you.

MY text contains the apostle's valediction on the Church of Corinth. And a very affectionate and pathetic one it is; evidently proceeding, from a heart warm with divine love, and containing great encouragement to the person, who, cordially complies with the exhortation therein contained. It seems, it was anciently, as it now is, customary for an author to conclude his epistle with a benevolent with. Paul falls in with this custom the more readily, as it fruits the present temper of his heart. He does not take his leave with a dry empty compliment, but heartily wishes the Corinthians the best blessing, which is the divine special presence, which he also promises them on their compliance with the exhortation. This consists of several short sentences. Be perfect, Katartizes the, literally it signifies be compact, or united, which is as the members of the same body, or the constitute parts of the same building. The perfection of a society lies much in the unity of it. It is probable, that the apostle here, has particular reference to the perfection or completing the body of the Corinthian Church, by restoring some members, who had for a time been separated from its communion by suspension; or else who had, by a divine contentious spirit, withdrawn themselves. The original word quoted favors this sense, signifying the putting those members of a body into their proper places, which had been loosened from their joint. Be of good comfort: the original word may be rendered exhorted, or comforted, or confined; what if we should take it as comprehending all these? Be exhorted to pay a due regard to the various precepts and counsels I have given you from the spirit of God. Be comforted in all the trials, all the afflictions you have met, or may meet with your profession of the gospel. Be confirmed which is in the truths and righteous ways of God. Be of one mind; q. d. labor for a unity of sentiment; try to think alike, to be of the same mind, of the same judgment, in matters of religion; but if you cannot attain to this, but are obliged to deliver in opinion in some lesser things, yet be one in affection, live in peace: i.e. free from that wrath and envy, those contentions and strife's, which have hitherto been but to frequent among you; remember that the wrath of man worketh not the righteousness of God; and do not by your conduct, give me occasion to repeat these words; " whereas there be divisions among you, are ye not carnal, and walk as men." To induce to a ready compliance with the duty exhorted to, he adds, the God of love and peace shall be with you: q. d. The truth God is the God of peace; he is love in the abstract, so that your complying with this exhortation is the direct way to enjoy his gracious spiritual presence. What an animating motive is here!

In speaking more largely on this subject, I shall endeavor,

First to show what that peace and love among Christians is, to which the apostle exhorts with so much warmth and earnestness.

Secondly, to evince and illustrate the great importance of such a peace, among Christians, those particularly, who are connected in the same society.

Thirdly, adventure to give a few directions, by a due attendance on which, this important blessing may be attained and promoted among Christians. And then make some application.

I am to show first, what that peace and love among Christians is, to which the apostle exhorts with so much warmth and earnestness? In answer to this enquiry, I shall mention two essential characters or qualifications of this peace.

First, an agreement in principle, at least in the main things. The prophet no doubt intends, that his question should have an answer, when he says, can two walk together except they be agreed? (Amos 3. 3.) Doubtless two may walk together, i.e. may have religious fellowship; may join sweet counsel, who differ in sentiments on some lesser points, otherwise there could be no act of occasional communion, among Christians of different denominations: Nay, perhaps, it would be found on enquiry, that there could be no such thing as religious fellowship or walking together, in the matters of religion, but every one must walk by himself, there not being two persons, who are exactly agreed in all points of doctrine. In matters of lesser moment, Christians should exercise mutual forbearance: a tender, charitable disposition, towards a Christian brother, erring in some lesser things, will be an effect of that modesty and humility, which well becomes the present infant state of darkness and imperfection, where the best know but in part, and all are liable to error. To see the Christian Church rent to pieces, by the over rigid urging of uniformity, in sentiment and practice, on points of small moment; and persons under the influence of party rage, excommunicating and anathematizing one another, as though the essence of religion was at stake, affords a lively picture of human weakness and folly; and yet, how often do we see humbling and shameful instances of this kind; sometimes in men, who are, other ways, pious, learned, eminent.

But then all this is freely granted, in nevertheless remains true, that among Christians, particularly those, who are associated in religious societies, there should be an agreement in principle, at least in the main things. To see Orthodox, Arians, Pelagians, Socinians, and even Deists, all confusedly blended together in one communion, is not seemly. This may be termed Catholicism, but it is latitudinarianism. This is saying a confederacy, to which heaven will not say amen; and instead of being acceptable, is abominable to God. What fellowship hath light with darkness! It is surprising, as well as sad to observe, to what a length some moderns have carried the matter, even to the asserting, that it is no material thing, what a man's religious opinions are, provided, he appear to be of a benevolent disposition, and to pay a proper regard to the social virtues. This is departing from bigotry, a worse extreme. Christians should beware of all extremes: they should remember, that the wisdom which cometh from above, is first pure, then peaceable: that precious as peace is, they who sell the truth to buy it, give too high a price. If they consult their Bibles, they may read of damnable heresies (2 Peter 2. 1.), doctrines, that subvert souls (Acts 15. 24), words, that eat like a canker (2 Tim 2. 17.), Among all the apostles of our Lord, none was more eminent for a Catholic disposition, a heart dilated with the love of God, than the apostle John: and yet, how strict he is upon the head of doctrine, you see, by that precept, 2 Epis. of John, 9. 10, whosoever transgresseth, and bring not this doctrine, receive him not unto your house, neither bid him God speed; for he that biddeth him God speed, is a partaker of his evil deeds. How awful are those words of Paul, Gal. 1. 8. where, he is manifestly speaking of those, who, in the justification of a sinner, mingled the law with the gospel. Through we are an angel from Heaven, profess any other gospel unto you, than that ye have received, let him be accursed.

Secondly, another essential character or qualification of that peace among Christians, which the apostle exhorts to in my text, is, that it be founded on love to God. There may be, and often is an external peace, among a professed Christians, and much outward unity and harmony, where there is little or nothing of the love of God at bottom. Such a peace may be founded upon principles of policy, or on a party spirit. "We must be united, this will render us a respectable body; nothing will be able to stand against us; we shall be an over-match for all our adversaries." Thus many reason; and this is the basis of their strict union. But this is not the peace and love, which my text so warmly recommends. There is nothing peculiar to Christianity in this peace. A society of Mahometans or Pagans, may keep united from the same motives, the same political views. The peace and love in my text, is built on love to God: according to that divine word, every one that loveth him also that is begotten of him (1 John 5. 1.). That love which unites true believers to the head, cements them in the closet, and most cordial bonds to each other. They regard one another, as the children of one common father, who have one Lord, one faith, one baptism; who are one bread and one body; who are at present, in many respects in the same circumstances, in the same state of warfare and trial, exposed to the same enemies and temptations; who expect a common salvation. And hence they love as brethren, are pitiful and courteous, no one allows himself to seek his own good, separate from that of his brethren. They cover one another's infirmities with love: they feel the happy and powerful influence of that servant charity, which is bound of perfectness; and hence, they do all mutual good offices, with a benevolent heart. Happy the Christian society, which is held together by this bond!

I proceed to the second head, i. e. to show, of how great importance, such a peace and harmony as has been described, is among Christians, those particularly, who are connected in the same society.

That such peace and love is a valuable and important blessing to Christian societies appears from the warm manner, in which it is urged in my text, and other scriptures; and the powerful motives with which the duty is enforced. How affectionate is the apostles in the text; how warm, and withal, how argumentative! Those are pathetic words, Phil. ii. 1, 2. "If there be therefore any consolation in Christ, if any bowels and mercies: fulfill ye my joy, that ye be like minded, having the same love, being of one accord, of one mind." In what a variety of expression, does the prince of peace recommend love and peace to his followers? This is his "new commandment" (John 13. 34.). This is the badge, or distinguishing note of his disciples (ver. 25.). May I not add that this is one of the things which our great intercessor is now pleading for, on the behalf of his people, at the throne of grace? This we may learn, from that specimen he gave his intercession, before his passion; see John 17. 21. "That they all may be one, as thou father art in me, and I in thee, that they also may be one in us; that the World may know that thou hast sent me, and hast loved them as thou hast loved me." To excite them to peace and love, he puts them in mind that they are brethren, that they are but a little flock, have many and formidable enemies; that therefore, they should cleave close together. I might show that love is called the fulfilling of the law; (Rom 13. 8.) is put among the foremost of the fruits of the spirit. (Gal. 6. 22.) The apostle John, who is termed by way of eminence, "the disciple whom Jesus loved", and who partook of our Lord's spirit in a eminent degree, appears transported in a manner, in the commendation of Christian love and unity. "Love (says he) is of God, and every one that loveth, is born of God, and knoweth God." That "he who dweleth in love, dwelleth in God, and God in him." That he who is destitute of love, whatever other attainments he may boast of, is "a murderer, a liar, and abideth in death." It is reported of this apostle that as he survived all the rest, and lived to extreme old age, so when his powers were greatly enfeebled, in so much, that he could do little more than move and speak a few words, he often used to address the Christians, saying, "see that ye love one another." I might moreover show, that Christians are commanded "to be kindly affectioned one to another: That love be without dissimulation: To be pitiful and courteous: To provoke one another to love and to good works."

   Now considering how express the scripture is upon this head, I think, there are but few duties of religion, the obligation of which is more difficult to evade. If a person be utterly destitute of love, be evidently of a sour, narrow, selfish, malevolent temper; if he be under the dominion of a malicious, revengeful spirit; what even knowledge he has, what ever faith, what ever zeal for God and his truth, he may pretend to, it is plain, that the love of God has never taken possession of his heart. If it had it would doubtlessly have humbled his pride, and molded him into a more Christ like temper. A society in which there is little or no brotherly love to be seen, where jealousies and heart burnings, bitter envying and strife, whispering and backbitings are frequent, is more like a society of Pagans than Christians.

"Living in malice and envy, hateful and hating one another," was a character suitable to the gentiles, before they know Christ; "but after that the kindness and love of God our savior towards man appeared," and they began to feel the benign influence of the Christian religion, matters put on a new face. (Tit. 3. 3, 4.)

I might here expatiate, in showing the excellency and importance of love. It were easy to make it appear, that love is the very spirit of angels, of glorified saints, and of the best men upon Earth. Perhaps there is nothing, wherein the distinguished, as by love and goodness. The Devils have spiritual immortal natures, and great degrees of power and knowledge, but Devils cannot love; instead of love, sweetness and benignity, with which the blessed angels are replete, these depraved lost, miserable spirits, are subject to the vassalage of fierce passion of malice, cruelty and revenge. "These are the very image of Satan, and the spirit of Hell." On the other hand, we have reason to think, that the blessed angels and glorified saints live in the joyful exercise of perpetual love, and the most tender endearments: and the better any man is upon Earth, the nearer he approaches to the temper of the blessed inhabitants above. Love dilates the good man's heart, so that he no longer makes himself his chief end, but he has a sincere concern for the good of others. It is one of the characters of charity, that "she seeketh not her own." (Cor. 13.) The good man is never so much pleased, as when he is employed as an instrument, in the hand of God, in promoting the good of others; he shows mercy with cheerfulness. How many lovely examples of this kind, does the sacred scriptures afford, as well as later history. Oh that there were more of them! Oh that the same mind might be in us, which also was in Christ Jesus?

I might add, that, as love is the spirit of angels, and good men, so it is the tie or band of Christian communion. This communion is necessary, at least, for the well-being of the church, which is a compound body, made up of many parts or members, which stand in mutual need of one another; the qualifications or gifts of this member, supplying the defects of that; each contributing its part, to the good of the whole: so that "the eye cannot say to the hand, nor the head to the foot, I have no need of thee." Now, in a divided state, where love is gone, and instead of keeping the unity of the spirit, in the bond of peace, a Christian society is split into parties, a sad consequence often is, that they who should lay out their talents for the good of the body, are apt to employ them for its hurt. Instead of edifying or building up, they do their utmost to pull down with both hands. It is an observation which has been often made, and which is a sad truth, that the greatest evils which have befallen Christian societies, are those which flow from intestine divisions, growing upon the decay of love. That these are the flames which have consumed the church, when the flames of persecution have only singed her garments.

I might add, that love and peace in Christian societies, commends Christianity to them that are without. Behold how the Christians Love one another, was a proverb among the heathen in the primitive times; and I make no doubt, but the seeing this sweet harmony, was the means of convincing many a spectator, of gaining proselytes. I have often thought, that were the humility, the goodness, the peaceableness and charity of the Christian religion transcribed, or carefully copied into the lives of its professors, it could scarcely fail of captivating the hearts of impartial spectators. They would be ready to say, "surely this religion must needs be from God, which makes its professors so Godlike." And in consequence hereof, they would be apt to take up the same happy resolution, with those mentioned by the prophet, who said, "We will go with you, for we have heard that God is with you." (John 17. 21.) Hence our skillful intercessor, when he pleads for unity among his disciples, use this argument that hereby the whole World would be convinced, that his mission was from God, or that Christianity had a divine original. "That they all may be one, as thou father art in me, and I in thee, that they may also be one in us, that the World may believe that thou hast sent me." (Zach 8. 23.) What is the reason why Christianity makes so little progress in the World, not withstanding of many excellent books, and much good preaching, and other precious means! Alas, the reason, or at least one main reason, is the bitter party spirit, the fierce tempers, the antichristian live of many of its professors: these are the things which powerfully tend to harden the profane in their evil ways, and to cast a stumbling block in the way of the blind.

I might further add, that where there is in a Christian society, such a peace as has been described, its salutary effects are innumerable. The apostle James observes, that "where envying and strife is, there is confusion and every evil work." So on the other hand, where there is love and peace of the right sort, there, will be every good work, for love is the fulfilling of the law. For instance, the member of such a society, will be mutually assisting to each other, in all difficulties; they will help to "bear one another's burdens, and so to fulfill the law of Christ." If anything is projected, tending to promote the common good, it meets with a general suffrage, is harmoniously embraced. Whereas in a divided state, one party is apt to oppose, what the other projects, so that the salutary scheme is rejected, and the common interest suffers. Where there is love between a minister and people, where he knows he has their hearts, and that he is heard with candor and due respect, it cheers his spirits, and encourages him to deliver his message with precision, with life, with tenderness, on the contrary, when an evil spirit is got between pastor and flock, so that he has reason to suspect he is hated or despised, it is apt to embarrass his mind, and so to discourage him, as that it is well if he does not resolve, that he will make no more mention of the name of the Lord. Let what has been said, suffice as to the excellency of love and peace, and its happy influence among Christians, especially them that are connected in the same society.

The third and last part in the doctrinal part, was to give a few directions by attending to which, Christians may receive some assistance, in putting in practice the apostolical exhortation in my text. This, however unfit for, I shall attempt with all humility, in the following particulars, in which I request a candid hearing.

I. Let Christians, who would enjoy peace, and live in love, look and apply to him, with whom is the residue of the spirit, for a revival of religion. To have it revived in their own hearts, and in the societies to which they belong. The essence of religion is love. Love to men, originating from a principle of love to God, is "the fulfilling of the law", and I might add the gospel also. And, as a love to the brethren, is founded on love to God, so when the latter is decayed, the former cannot be expected to flourish. Sometimes this is remarkably the case. The great interesting matters of eternity are in a sad degree out of sight. The effect of which is, that the love of many is waxed cold. The forgiving love, and astonishing grace of God, manifested in the gospel, has but a feeble influence on the hearts of professors. Christians, at such a time, can hear the truths of religion, and perhaps approve of them in their speculative judgment, but they do not relish the truth, they do not feel it. They do not "receive the truth in the love of it." In a word, the things that remain are ready to die; inward godliness is in a low state. A wasting consumption preys on her vitals, by which the glory of Jacob is made thin, and the fatness of his flock is waxed lean. Now, when this is the case, there is apt to be but little brotherly love, very little of that fervent charity, which is the bond of perfectness. A private selfish spirit is apt to prevail. That lovely character of charity is forgot, which is that she seeketh not her own. Everyone acts as if he were made for himself only. People at such times, are easily offended, and hard to be reconciled; their passions, touched with the smallest spark, are apt to fly into the most furious and violent explosions. They are ready to take one another by the throat for a very trifle. "I'll not let it go with him, I'll be revenged on him, I'll do to him as he has done to me, I'll render to the man according to his work." O sirs, where the prince of peace appears among a people, with the precious influence of his special grace, this private, selfish, this fierce vindictive spirit, falls before him, as Dagon fell before the ark of God. Christians would be disposed to embrace one another; to love as brethren; and notwithstanding some lesser differences, to keep "the unity of the spirit, in the bond of peace."

II. Get the inward corruptions of the heart subdued. You may remember the question of the apostle James, with the answer; "Whence come wars and fightings? Come they not hence, even of your lusts that war in your members?" There is a spirit naturally in man that lusteth to envy. Men are naturally of a revengeful disposition. I might also mention pride: this makes men impatient of contradiction, Scorn to give place to any disposes them to set up their wills, to regard their own judgment, as the standard to which all must conform. Pride is so many ways destructive to the peace of society, that the wise man sees ground for that observation, "Only by pride cometh contention." (Prov 14. 10.) If professors would live in peace, and enjoy peace in the societies they belong to, they should endeavor to find out these corruptions of the heart to lament them; to spread them before the physician of souls, in order to a cure; to beg of him that "through the spirit they may be helped to mortify the deeds of the body.

III. Avoid any conduct, which tends to render each other odious. This is a shameful behavior in the disciples of Christ; directly contrary to that charity, without which, we are as " a sounding brass, and tinkling cymbal." And yet I appeal to facts, whether it be not too common among professors, especially when a party spirit runs high. Sirs, we should carefully shun every practice of this kind. We should beware of party names, such as new lights, old lights, new schemers, opposers, &c. These things tend to irritate and inflame men's spirits, and by this means to widen divisions. Do not be forward in condemning one another as heretics or putting the worst meaning on every doubtful expression, thereby making a man an offender for a word. Do not impute to your neighbors all those consequences, which you think are fairly deducible, from some principle of his, providing you find, that he professes not to see these consequences to be the result of his principle. That far from owning the consequence, he detests it as much as you do; and declares, that he would renounce the principle, if he were convinced, that it did really give ground for any such consequence. When will Christians learn to treat one another with candor!

IV. Be on your guard against whisperers and tale bearers. The Devil is the accuser of the brethren; (Rev 12. 10.) He might also be called the accuser of God, for he accuses God to men, as well as men to God; and he accuses men to men. And as Satan loves to sow discord, so are there not some of mankind that do in this particular too nearly resemble him? Solomon observes, that a "forward man soweth strife, and a whisperer separateth chief friends. (Prov 16. 28.)" Some are like the troubled sea that cannot rest; those talents, in a right improvement of which, they might do much good, they employ in doing mischief. Instead of acting the part, and deserving the character of peace-makers, they act the part of incendiaries. They employ themselves in the odious office of tale-bearers. Such persons, far from being encouraged, should be regarded as the pests of society, and treated with the neglect and contempt they deserve. And if they were thus hated, they would soon loose their influence, and grow weary of their hateful employment; and thus the remark of the wise man would be verified, "The north wind driveth away rain, so doth an angry countenance a back-biting tongue." (Prov 25. 23.) It is the encouragement that is given to such, especially by persons in public stations, which tends greatly to increase the number of these pernicious vermin, as well as to wet their diabolical zeal; and so, another remark of Solomon, is sadly verified, that "when a ruler hearkens to lies, all his servants are wicked." (Prov 29. 13.)

V. Be not forward to enter into disputes, upon controverted points. I grant that debating a point fairly, has often a good tendency to the investigation of truth, but as disputes are managed, there is seldom much good comes of them, and often a great deal of mischief. How often they seen to end in vain jangling and bitter altercation! How frequently do the parties in a controversy leave the point in debate, and fall to pelting one another with virulent personal reflections! If at anytime we debate a point, let it be with that moderation, that coolness and candor, which may make it appear that it is truth, not victory we have in view. Never cast dirt, never so anything that might but seem to favor of hatred or contempt of the person of antagonist. Never think it a shame, but account it your honor to give up a point, when you are convinced it cannot be defended. And be candid enough to own your error, as soon as you are convinced you are in error. If you find that disputes cannot be managed without envy, strife, evil surmisings, and the like, then avoid them altogether. Remember, that "the wrath of man worketh not the righteousness of God."

VI. Beware of a false and irregular zeal. True zeal, under a proper regimen, is indeed a very lovely grace. "Be zealous," was one part of the advice of the spirit, to the wretched Church of Laodiciea (Laodicea). There can be no true religion without this grace. Fervency in spirit is a necessity qualification in the service of God. We have zeal recommended, by the example of our Lord; his amiable moderation, and lamblike meekness, had no tendency to take off the edge of zeal. Hence, he says, the zeal of thy house hath eaten me up." For the want of this grace Christ threatens to spew Laodicea out of his mouth. "It is good to be zealously affected, always, in a good thing." But how excellent so ever zeal is, it is a grace which requires a heavy ballast. Dreadful have been the effects which false zeal has produced. How often have persons, under the influence of it, spoken wickedly for God and talked deceitfully for hi,. It made a conscientious persecutor of Saul the Pharisee; (Acts 26. 9.) nor was he the only instance of the kind: "They shall put you out of the synagogue (saith Christ) yea the time cometh, that whosoever killeth you, shall think that he doeth God service." (John 16. 2.) The false teachers in the church of Galatia, who stirred up the Christians against Paul, their spiritual father, zealously affected them, but not well. (Gal 4. 17.)

If zeal is not found in conjunction with truth; if it is not guided by wisdom, and qualified by the Christian temper; the more zeal a person has, the worse; the more mischief is he like to do.

VII. Be on your guard against a separating spirit. This is an antichristian spirit. Separates often talk much of the spirit, and make high pretences to it; but let them pretend what they will, it will be found on enquiry that want of the spirit of Christ is at the bottom of their conduct. See Jude 19 ver. "These be they who separate themselves, sensual, having not the spirit." The Jewish church in the days of our Lord was become very corrupt; and yet, he countenanced her so far, as to attend her ordinances, common and special. And it is hard to name anything, which the heart of Christ appears to be more set upon, than that his disciples might be united among themselves. It has been observed of some eminently godly men, ministers and others, that in experience and sanctification, so they have been more and more tender of the churches peace, and fearful of division. I would by no means have anything that I have said, be so understood, as if I condemned all separations: some are no doubt lawful, and matter of duty. Such was the separation of our fathers from mystical Babylon, the mother of harlots, and abomination of the Earth. If a professing church is gone off from the gospel of Christ, to another gospel; if the gospel way of sinner's justification is not taught; if mans supposed sincere obedience, is put in the room of Christ's righteousness; if the necessity of faith and regeneration, are not insisted upon, or the true nature of them is explained away; if the special influences of the divine spirit are derided and denied; if the general strain of teaching in a church is evidently legal, such as in the nature of it tends to settle sinners on the covenant of works, instead of disposing them to renounce all confidence in the flesh; in a word, if a church corrupt the word of God, and reject or neglect the means of purging herself, with Babylon refusing to be healed, in this case the Lord seems to call for a separation. See the command, 2 Cor. 6. 17. "Wherefore, come out from among them, and be ye separate, faith the Lord, and touch not the unclean thing, and I will receive you." Or if a church, which is doctrinally sound in the main things, impose on her members' unscriptural terms of communion; so that they cannot be of her communion without wounding and defiling the conscience, by doing that which is sinful, in this case separation seems inevitable. We are never to do evil that good may come. "Whatsoever is not of faith, is sin." This was the case of those, who dissented from the Episcopal Church in South Britain and Ireland. But for the members of a church to separate, where they do not allege, that an unscriptural or sinful terms of communion are imposed; where they cannot deny but the doctrine is sound, and the true way of salvation is taught, because they think the minister's gifts are not quite so edifying, that he is not so zealous, so lively, so spiritual, so evangelical as some others, or that he has not so happy a talent in distinguishing, or riding marches between the law and the gospel. Or to separate, because it is alleged that there are some corrupt members in a church; that she does not exercise discipline with that impartiality and strictness that might be wished; these are separations, to which Heaven will not give its sanction. How many, who seem more fearful of being defiled by corruptions of their own hearts! These would do well to remember that it is "out of the heart that divers abominations proceed; (Mat. 4. 19.) that "these are the things which defile a man;" that "he who eateth and drinketh unworthily, eateth and drinketh damnation to himself." (1 Cor. 11. 29.) Such conduct as we are faulting has rendered the ancient Donatists infamous in the future ages of the Christian church. ("Donatists, I find, had their name from Donatus. He lived about the time of the emperor Constantine. The real cause of his going off from the church is said, to be a discontent that he missed of the bishopric of Carthage. He would allow no church to be a true church, but what was pure from all sin. He rebaptised those who had been baptized by them whom he called heretics") I do not find that they are charged with any gross doctrinal error; schism was their crime. The church was too corrupt for them to abide in her fellowship. They presented to set up pure churches. By their unchargable breaches of communion, they rent to pieces the seamless coat of our Lord. Their hateful practices tended to destroy that unity, which renders the church "fair as the moon, clear as the sun, and terrible as an army with banners." They were active in exposing their mother's nakedness, which final duty bound them to conceal. They repeated the crime of Noah's impious grandson, on account of which the patriarch pronounced these terrible prophetic words, "cursed be Canaan, a servant of servants shall he be to his brethren"

VIII. Beware of false teachers. The Church of Ephesus is commended for "trying them, who said they were apostles, and finding them liars." (Rev. 2. 2.) The apostle John cautions the Christians not to believe every spirit, but "to try the spirits whether they be of God." (1. John 4. 1.) The Christian people have the more need to be on their guard against such, because no age of the church is exempt from them. Sometimes they abound greatly and perhaps never more, than in a day of God's power. If Satan cannot prevent God's work, he will endeavor to mimic, and by this means, to bring a slur upon it. When Moses did, by the power of God work true, the magicians, by the assistance of Satan, wrought counterfeit miracles. So in the apostle's days, there were false apostles. So at the reformation, how were the bowels of the infant church, in a manner torn to pieces, by the divisive practices of Anabaptists, and other enthusiasts.

People should beware of the depths of Satan; they have more need, considering that false teachers do often act with much cunning, so that the hurt they do is not presently discerned. Hence they are compared to foxes, to "little foxes, that spoil the tender vine." (Can. 2. 15.) They often make a fair show, hence they are said to come "in sheep's clothing." (Mat. 7. 15.) And are called "deceitful workers transforming themselves into the apostles of Christ." Some of them are said you show great signs and wonders, to deceive, were it possible, the very elcet. Such teachers may have rich natural endowments, and great acquirements; they may preach many precious truths; they may be soft and insinuating in their address; may profess great intimacy with Heaven; they may not only use such good words and fair speeches, as have a tendency to deceive, but may make high pretences to zeal, and may zealously affect their easy credulous followers; and they do this the more easily, because as their principal design (whatever they may pretend to the contrary) is to please, rather than to edify; so they are apt to fall in which men's favorite passions, by insisting chiefly on such topics as they know will please. In sine, to discern between true and false teachers is not so easy a thing as some may imagine, especially at a time when a sectarian spirit prevails; when unclean spirits ascend as it were in swarms, out of the bottomless pit; when many false prophets are gone out into the World; when there are a great variety of opposite pretences, one crying, "lo here is Christ," and another, lo he is there, and each very sanguine that he is in the right, and that he is only so. But is deception then unavoidable" Is there no criterion, no certain mark, by which God's people may avoid being deceived; by which, the sheep of Christ may be able to discern his voice, from the choice of strangers? Yes, blessed be God there is, else our Lord could not have said, "by their fruits ye shall know them." (Mat. 7.) If a teacher does not direct souls to Christ, but to Moses for salvation; or, if under the notion of exalting Christ and grace, he teach what tends to licentiousness: if he is not open and frank: is not willing to declare his principles on all points: If he depreciate human learning and a regular induction into the gospel ministry: if the spirit he promotes among his followers, instead of a meek, humble, Catholic, be a violent, furious, self sufficient spirit: if he acts deceitfully, pretending one thing, when it is evident he intended another, disclaiming and pretending to abhor a party spirit, when it appears more and more plain, that the promoting of a party spirit, was, and is the chief thing he had, and has in view: if they are active in endeavoring by every means, to pick members out of those churches, which themselves cannot deny to be true churches of Christ: if their whole conduct as far as it succeeds, evidently tends to build their own sect, on the ruins of every other denomination of professed Christians: if under the highest pretences to disinterestedness, they are evidently greedy of filthy lucre, or, if they are strangers, and not properly recommended; in any or all of these cases, people would do well to fear the worst, and to act with caution. That is a very solemn and tender address of the apostle, Rom. 16. 17, 18. "Now, I beseech you brethren, mark them which cause divisions and offences, contrary to the doctrine ye have learned, and avoid them, for they that are such, serve not our Lord Jesus Christ, nut their own belly, and with good words and fair speeches, deceives the hearts of the simple."

Having gone through the doctrinal part, I proceed to some practical improvement, which, I have in a great measure anticipated by what has been said, particularly on the last general head. I shall therefore confine what I add, to a use of lamentation, and a few words of exhortation.

First, I say, we may infer from the subject, that the divisions among Christians are much to be lamented. How many parties at this day, each very sanguine that they are in the right; one crying, lo here is Christ, and another, lo he is there! Professors not only divide, but subdivide, crumbled almost into atoms of parties, "Ephraim against Manasseh, and Manasseh against Ephraim, and they together against Judah." In how many places, Where hopeful religious appearances have been of late, have tares sprung up, almost to the choking of the good seed. Surely an enemy hath done this? And yet, are not such enemies, by many mistaken for friends. None so high in the esteem of some, as those who run into the difficult office of the ministry, without being sent; who would be teachers of the law and the gospel too, not knowing what they say, nor whereof they affirm. Are not persons of this stamp hugged and caressed, while the faithful ministers of Christ are despised? None like those who go about as incendiaries, endeavoring to fill the minds of people with prejudices against human learning and a regular ministry: who deal with mankind, rather as affectionate than rational creatures, using their skill to get the passions of people on their side, that by the means of them, they bribe the judgment, and so win proselytes to their party. Are there not in our days, persons of the same complexion, with those mentioned by the apostle, who "creep into houses, and lead captive silly women," and men also? And in some places, do not people seem to be seized with a spiritual giddiness; like a ship without ballast, are tossed with every wind; appear possessed with an incessant desire of novelty; with the Athenians, seeking to "hear some new thing, heaping to themselves teachers, having itching ears, ever learning, and never able to look awful to see many, and some of whom better might have been expected, renouncing their infant baptism? Others pretending to be the only Christians, according to the primitive model, representing all other denominations, as corrupters of the word of God, and their teachers, as blind leaders of the blind; while the carnally secure, and men of infidel principals, or of a deistical turn, make a scoff at all these things, and ridicule Christianity itself, on account of the folly of its professors. Surely sirs, these divisions of rulers, are sufficient ground for great thoughts of heart. I know but of one consideration, which upon such a proposition is sufficient to quiet the mind of him, who prefers the welfare of Zion to his chief joy. It is this that all things are in the hands of Zion's king: that he hath power and skill sufficient to bring a revenue of glory to God, even from human weakness and folly. Oh that the ecclesiastical anarchy of this day might dispose ministers and other Christians, to enter into a serious enquiry, whether a common sense about the churches might not be likely to present many of these bad things, and to keep out the boar of the forest, from entering in to waste the vineyard at his pleasure.

I proceed to a word of exhortation. First, to the unconverted. Although I would have you to take a part of the advise of the apostle in my text, i.e. to live in peace with men, yet that which chiefly concerns you, is to get into a state of reconciliation or peace with God. Consider, that till once you are in this state, you cannot love your neighbor, nor do any duty you owe to him from a right principle. Some of you, are already, it may be, in possession of a sort of peace: "The strong man armed, keepeth his place, and his goods are in peace." But does not your own conscience tell you that your peace is not well founded? That it will not endure the test of God's word? That you have never been awakened, convinces and humbled? That the spirit of self dependence has never been effectually subdued? That you have never gone out of yourself to Christ; that you are not new creatures, so that if you die in your present state, you must needs perish? To such I would say; why will you, or rather how can you remain easy in your present state? Can you think with any patience, of falling into the hands of the iniquity, and having your portion with the unclean? Nay, can you bear the thought of having the hottest place in Hell; of sinking far deeper than the abominable Sodomites, in the lake that burns with fire and brimstone? If you cannot, then "acquaint yourselves with God and be at peace," take hold of this strength and make peace;" and what you do quickly; to delay till tomorrow, may be forever too late. The axe is laid to the root of the tree, and the judge stands at the door. "Your judgment for a longtime lingereth not, and I trust yet is in many places, a day of God's power. Such seasons do not happen often: if you outstand this, you may never see another. They are everlasting words, Jer. 8. 20. "The harvest is past, the summer is ended, and we are not saved."

May I, without offence, be permitted to drop a word to ministers? I would just say, let us, my dear brethren, pray for the peace of Jerusalem, and do what we can to promote it. If we would put an effectual stop to men of separating principles and practices, let us out do them in abundant labors in evangelical preaching, in zeal for God, and hearty concern for souls. To use bishop burnets words, in his pastoral letter to his clergy, "let us out preach them, out pray them, and out live them." I would add, let us see that we hurt not the churches peace, nor lay a stumbling block in the way of our people, by carrying Catholicism too far. For instance if they see us giving the right hand of fellowship to men of corrupt principles, will not this be a cause of stumbling to them? How natural will it be for them to say, these our teachers inculcate on us the absolute sovereignty and freedom of divine grace, the doctrine of original sin, of justification by faith only, of the new birth, of the necessity of divine supernatural influence, &c. but we see that they maintain all acts of communion with those, that do not believe these doctrines. What can we infer from this their conduct, but either, they do not believe these doctrines, or at least, do not believe them to be important as they teach us they are. Perhaps, some of us are not sufficiently aware, how stumbling this is to some of our hearers, and what a handle is made of it by separates.

To the assembly in general, I would say, you have been hearing in the doctrinal part of the nature of that peace which is acceptable to God. What an excellent and important blessing it is: some directions have likewise been given by a due attendance on which, you may be likely to attain this invaluable blessing. These things, however weakly spoken upon, have been laid before you, I trust, with a single eye, by one who is under infinite obligations to redeeming love, and who has a sincere concern for the peace and welfare of Jerusalem. I hope then, you will take the word of instruction and exhortation in good part; and that you will follow with your earnest prayers, him who takes his affectionate leave of you, in the words of my text; "finally brethren farewell; be perfect, be of good comfort, be of one mind, live in peace, and the God of love and peace shall be with you."

F I N I S.

An ISRAELITE indeed

A

SERMON,

Occasioned by the DEATH of

The Rev. Mr. JOHN MOORHEAD;

Preached at the Presbyterian CHURCH in BOSTON,

To the bereaved FLOCK,

The first SABBATH after his FUNERAL.

By DAVID McGREGORE, A.M.
PASTOR of a CHURCH in LONDONDERRY.

Mark the perfect Man, and behold the upright, for the end of that Man is Peace. PSAL. XXXVII. 37.

Integer vitae sceleris que purus Non eget, &c.

[PUBLISHED AT THE DESIRE OF THE HEARERS.]

BOSTON:

Printed and Sold by William McAlpine,
In Marlborough Street.
M,DCC,LXXIV.

An ISRAELITE indeed

A Funeral SERMON

JOHN 1. 47.

....*Behold an Israelite indeed, in whom is no guile.*

PON the news of the death of your loved pastor, together with your invitation to keep the Sabbath with you on that mournful occasion, the text now read came repeatedly into my mind.

To throw together a few hasty thoughts upon it, is all that the short time, and other circumstances would allow. In which, though I do not expect to please curious, critical, dainty hearers, yet I am not without hope of saying something that may prove a word in season, to serious, hungry, weeping Christians.

The sacred historian in the context gives an account of the calling of Philip.

On the manner and circumstances of this call, at present, I shall not detain you. I shall only notice, that Philip, coming to know Christ savingly, is all impatience, till he have communicated the precious and important discovery to his friend Nathaniel.

Carnal men are for monopolizing the riches of the World; they would have all to themselves. Is it so with respect to spiritual riches? Quite the reverse.

The happy person who has found Christ, would gladly have his friends, his acquaintance, have all to come and be joint partners; or as it is expressed, heirs together of the grace of life

We find Nathaniel at first, objecting against Philip's important discovery, in these words, can one good thing come out of Nazareth? If Nathaniel by this objection, means that the Messiah could not come out of Nazareth, so far he was right; for he knew, or might know from the scriptures, that the Messiah was to come out of Bethlehem. But if Nathaniel's objection arose from a rooted prejudice against Nazareth, as a place so mean, so obscure and contemptible, that nothing good or great, or excellent could be expected to come out of it, (as some are prejudiced against this place, that city, or nation,) herein he was wrong.

Efficacious grace can, and often does produce excellent pieces of workmanship from the meanest materials.

We find that Philip himself was as yet, ignorant of the true place of our Lord's nativity; thinking that he had really originated from Nazareth, and therefore could not fully remove Nathaniel's objection. But in answer to his question, he invites Nathaniel to come and see. q. d. my dear friend, let not you and I stand here arguing and raising difficulties, which neither of us can fully clear up; rather let us by joint consent go immediately to Jesus himself. I am confident that on covering with him, the difficulties which at present exercise our minds will soon vanish. If those persons who are full of prejudice against inward vital religion, would be prevailed upon to try and judge for themselves; if they would be persuaded to comply with the Psalmist's pathetic request, oh taste and see if the Lord is good; (Psal. 34. 5.) they would quickly change their mind; they would soon find that what they treated with contempt, was more to be desired than gold, than much fine gold; sweeter than honey, or the honey comb. (Psal. 19. 10.) But alas, such is the power of their unhappy prejudice that it is to be feared the most of mankind refuse to take this wholesome advice. Nathaniel however, is not one of that number. For anything that appears, he readily accepted of Philip's invitation, and went with him to Jesus.

The sacred history informs us, that Jesus seeing Nathaniel coming, meets him with that honorable character in my text; saying publicly, and in Nathaniel's hearing, behold an Israelite indeed, in whom is no guile. We are told Rom. ix. 6. that they are not all Israelites, which are of Israel. And elsewhere, we have a distinction between Jesus outwardly, and Jews inwardly. (Rom. 2. 28, 29.) The character given of Nathaniel by our Lord, implies that he was a Jew inwardly; which (if I mistake not,) is the same with an Israelite indeed.

Our Lord adds, in whom is no guile: I am not to criticize on the word guile; let it suffice to say, that it is an expression several times used in scripture, in a figurative sense. I take it here, as well as elsewhere, to signify duplicity or deceit. When our Lord says of Nathaniel, in whom is no guile, it is q. d. he is not one of those double persons, who pretended one thing, and intend another; but he is a plain, down right honest man; one whose inside is of a piece with his appearance; who's actions and heart do tally. We find the same character, Psal. 33. 2. We are not to understand the character, in any of these places, as if the persons were absolutely perfect; not in that high sense in which it belongs to the followers of the lamb in Heaven; of whom it is said, in their mouths was found no guile, for they are without fault before the throne of God; (Rev. 14. 5.) but in a lower sense. When our Lord says, behold him, it is q. d. take notice of him, so as to approve of him in your judgment; so as to imitate him in your practice, and in the temper of your heart; behold him as a wonder, as a rare sight, as kind of prodigy, at a time when there is too much paint, so much hypocrisy and deceit; so little truth in the inward part; so little simplicity and godly sincerity.

In speaking more largely on the subject, I shall endeavor.

First, to explain at a greater length, and with all, somewhat to illustrate the character in my text.

Secondly, to show the powerful and happy influence, which this character will be apt to have on a Christian, and particularly on a gospel minister.

And finally, to make some improvement suitable to the subject, and the present mournful occasion.

I am then in the first place, to examine more fully, and to illustrate the character in my text. The importance of this head would have required more time for mature thought. Nevertheless, with humble dependence on the father of lights, let us attempt some delineation.

By an Israelite indeed, if I take the matter right, is to be understood the same with what is meant in common speech, by a good man, a real Christian; one who has been the happy subject of a work of effectual grace. In a word, I take the character in my text to belong to a regenerate person, and to be peculiar to such a one. Let us suppose any unregenerate person, who pretends to the character of an Israelite indeed, and let us examine with what ground he makes this pretence. Perhaps he is one whom the World calls an honest man, and he may be so in a certain sense, but not in the strict sense, not in the sublime sense of my test. If honestly consists in rendering to all their dues, then it is a character which the unregenerate man has no just claim to. Either he is partial in the law, has an apparent regard to one precept, while he lives in the open violation of another; it may be abstains from filthiness of the flesh; but indulges filthiness of the spirit. For instance, will not be guilty of drunkenness or uncleanness; but will allow himself in malice and revenge. The several parts of his moral conduct are like the legs of the lame, not equal; he cannot with truth adopt the Psalmist's words, I have respect unto all thy commandments. (Psal. 109. 6.) Either this is the case, or if we suppose the unregenerate to go further, so as to pay an apparent regard to all second table duties; yet does he perform these duties

An Israelite indeed   147

from the heart? Is he carried above self-love? In the doing of them has he a supreme regard to God? Alas no! God is scarcely in all thoughts. He may from some sinister principle draw out his purse, but he does not draw out his soul to the needy; he is not a cheerful giver; so that he bestows alms without charity. To be brief, whatever good thing he does to his neighbor, he is under the influence of some sinister motive in the doing of it; so that he is really a double minded man in the fight of that eye which sees things as they are; so far is he from having any just claim to the character of an Israelite indeed, in whom is no guile. His best actions are destitute of the essence of virtue; have no real goodness in them; are so many splendid peccatasbining sins in the fight of the omniscient and holy lawgiver, who weigheth the spirits.

   In a word, whatever second table duty is not founded on the first table of God's holy law, is spurious. There can be no true love to God; he has no single eye to the divine glory in what he does. He does not so much as know what this means. It is impossible such a one should have any true love to God; for he has no true knowledge of him; he has never had that spiritual view of the glory of God, in the face of Jesus Christ, which attracts and captivates the heart. Hence he hates God; has an carnal mind, which is enmity against God. (Romans 8. 7) As the scripture phrase is, he does not like to retain God in his knowledge; (Romans 1. 28.) so far from this, that he says to God, depart from me, for I desire not the knowledge of thy ways. (Job 21. 14) It is granted that unregenerate men may make a show not only of morality, but of religion; yea some of them may be very exact in the duties of instituted worship. They may come before God as his own children come; may sit with them in the same seats; may ask of God the ordinances of justice; may take delight in approaching to God. (Isa. 63. 2.) The Pharisees fasted often, and made many prayers. But whatever appearance of religion may be in such persons, it is no more than appearance; it is hypocrisy at bottom; the heart is not right with God. For instance, the person may pretend to pray, but he has not knowledge of the true God, nor of Jesus whom he has sent. With the Athenians he ignorantly worships the unknown God who is near in his mouth, is far from his reins. (Jer. 12. 2) He may in prayer pretend to confess sin, to beg that God would separate his soul from the love of sin, but herein his heart and lips are at variance; for really he is not willing to part with sin; he cannot, or he will not do without it; he hugs the traitor in his bosom; wickedness is sweet to him, and he hides it under his tongue. (Job. xx 12) And hence no marvel, that his sacrifice is an abomination; his prayer sin. He may attempt covenant duties in a solemn manner; may got to the communion table, and there pretend to seal the contract, to give his hand to the Lord by a solemn oath; but is there not reason to fear that in an unregenerate person, all this is hypocrisy; that they only flatter God with their mouth, and lie to him with their tongue. (Psal. 78. 36.)

Let it suffice at present to say, that though an unregenerate person may perform all the outward acts of religion, as well as morality, yet there is no truth in the inward part; no gracious sincerity. The fountain is corrupt, the streams are of a piece; so that he does nothing to divine acceptance; has no claim to the character of an Israelite indeed. Such persons, whose consciences tell them they are unregenerate, might do well to consider with seriousness, Titus. 1. 15. Unto them that are defiled and unbelieving is nothing pure, but even their mind and conscience is defiled.

But a regenerate person through grace, has a just claim to character of an Israelite indeed. The happy person has a spiritual knowledge of the blessed God, which has conquered the native enmity of his heart; he is glad there is such a being as God; he cordially adopts the psalmist's words, but our God is in the heavens, he hath done whatsoever he pleased. (Psal. 115. 3.) He ever trusts in the divine sovereignty; sincerely rejoices to see himself of such a God. To contemplate the perfections of God, especially as a God of grace, is his favorite subject; he would give the created universe if he had it, to know more of God, to get nearer him, to love him in a higher degree. The law of his God is in his heart; he has received a new edition of it from the band of a Mediator; (Gal 3. 9.) ever since which, the yoke which was formerly galling, becomes lost and easy, so that the person finds it pleasant to draw in it. He feels in his heart the words of the beloved disciple, verily his commandments are not grievous; (Joh 5. 3.) through grace he can make the psalmist's words his own, O how love can make thy law, it is my study all the day; (Psa 114. 4.) yea he not only loves the divine law, but the purity of it is the formal reason of his love, as Psa. 119. 140. Thy word is very pure, therefore thy servant loveth it.

The person sees the stamp of divine authority on one precept, as well as another:; and hence his obedience is coextended with the commandment, which is exceeding broad. (Prd 159. 96.) Although the person fails of absolute flawless perfection, yet he does not contently rest short of it; perfection is the mark, the thing he has in his eye; he aspires after it with a generous ambition; he would fain be perfect, as his father in heaven is perfect; he forgets the things that are behind, and reaches forward; he is by no means satisfied with himself, unless on the most accurate and impartial imperfection, he finds he is making some sensible advances towards perfection. Moreover, his obedience is not like one who is sensible that the secret movements, or hidden springs of his whole moral conduct, are perfectly known to God: that all things are naked and opened unto the eyes of him, with whom we have to do. (Heb 4. 13.) I have no doubt but David was an Israelite indeed; we have a devotional sentence drop from him, which I think is very expressive of this character; the expression I refer to is 2 Sam. 7. 20, thou Lord knowest thy servant: He was glad that God knew his heart, which no hypocrite ever was or can be. The person not only does what God commands as to the matter of it, but he does it from a gracious principle of religious honor, and child like fear, and so can answer that divine demand, Mal. 1. 6. If I be a father, where is my honor; if a martyr, where is my fear? He knows from happy experience the difference between the spirit of a slave, and the spirit of a child; that the Son has made him free, and he is free indeed; (Joh 7. 36.) and happy consequence of this glorious liberty is, that being made free from sin, he becomes the servant of righteousness, and has his fruit unto holiness. The person cleaves to God and his law, with a cordial and cheerful subjection of whole soul, which no unregenerate man ever experienced. He is like the servant who being offered his liberty at the year of jubilee, would not accept of it; but chooses that his matter should carry him to the door post, and pierce his ear through with an awl, in token of his being servant forever. I might have added, that the person is one who has renounced his highest attainments; everything wrought in him, as well as done by him in point of merit, and acceptance with God. In a word, he is one of those who can say as Phil. 3. 19. We are the circumcision, which worship God in spirit, and rejoice in Christ Jesus, and have no confidence in the flesh.

Thus I have endeavored as I proposed, to give a delineation of the character in my text.

The second head was to show the powerful and happy influence, which such a character will be apt to have upon a Christian, and particularly on a gospel minister.

This head naturally divides itself into two parts: I shall endeavor to say something on each of these distinctly. With respect to Christians in general, I shall exemplify the influence which the character will be apt to have upon them, in a few particulars, among many. And,

1. It tends to bear up the Christian under the heaviest load of affection. If you would see this exemplified in a very striking instance, turn your eye upon Jeb; view his case; observe how thick the messengers of heavy tidings come; the last always with the worst news. See him striped of his great wealth; reduced from a state of opulency, to extreme indigency, all on the sudden; and what was heavier, his whole family of dear children violently cut off by one awful tremendous blow; see his poor body in the mean

time, covered with loathsome painful ulcers from head to foot; his wife instead of an help-meet, acting the part of a devil, by tempting him to shoot the arrow of scorn against the throne of God, and to make a desperate exit. His friends, through good men, yet from a mistaken apprehension of his café, stinging him with their keen reproaches; representing him as an odious hypocrite, thereby adding grief to him, whom God had already wounded. And what was heavier than all the rest, hear him crying under a heart-felt sense of the divine displeasure, the arrows of the almighty are in me, the poison whereof drinketh up my spirit; the terrors of God do set themselves in array against me (Job 6. 4.). In fine, if we talk a complex view of the whole case, it would seem that Job had a burden too heavy for a mortal, and that frail nature must needs sink; and yet Job did not sink; and if we enquire what was it supported him under all his complicated distress? We may find it in those words, Job 10. 7.0 Thou knowest I am not wicked; q. d. although I be a poor imperfect creature, and have abundant reason to abhor myself, yet O thou heart-searching and holy God, thou knowest I am not a hypocrite, am not a wicked man, as these my friends take me to be. Let a person with Job be conscious of integrity of heart; let him know that he loves God, and he will be able to bear up his head bravely above the highest surges; when the floods of great waters swell, they shall not overwhelm his soul. This consciousness of integrity has often made the happy subject of it, smile with agony; glory in tribulation, and greatly to rejoice, when for a season they were in heaviness, through manifold temptations. But,

2. The character in my text will naturally lead the person to a habitual, upright conduct. He lays it down as an incontestable maxim that he who walketh uprightly, walketh surely. And hence, let the case be what it will, the question with him is not, what is the most cunning step, or what seems best in a political view? What will be the most pleasing to that God who is delighted with truth in the single, and his whole body is full of light; he has this for rejoicing, the testimony of his conscience, that in simplicity, and godly sincerity, be has had his conversation in the world.

3. The character in my text is an excellent antidote against slavish fear. There is nothing so much intimidates a person, as a consciousness of guilt; an apprehension that all is not right within; that God is his enemy. Such an one, to use the scripture phrase, is in great fear, where no fear is; he is apt to look on all mankind as commissioned by God against him; and hence to say with Cain, every one that findeth me shall slay me; to that he starts at his own shadow; is afraid of the sound of a shaken leaf. On the other hand, let a man that his heart is right with God; that God in Christ, is his reconciled father and friend; and this knowledge furnishes him with undaunted fortitude; renders him bold as a lion. Let it be never so dark and stormy out of doors, it is lightsome and calm within; and hence, when he bears of evil tidings, his heart is fixed, trusting in the Lord (Psal. cxii). This steady trust makes him like Mount Zion, which at no time can be moved; (Psal. 125.) he feels the Psalmist's words, the Lord is my light and my salvation, whom shall I fear? The Lord is the strength of my life, of whom shall I be afraid? And a little after, through an host shall encamp against me, my heart shall not fear; though war should rise against me, in this will I be confident (Psal. 32. 1, 3.).

Other particulars I might insist on, but I hasten to the second branch of this general head, i. e. to show in some particulars, the happy influence the character in my text, will have on a gospel minister.

1. It will inspire him with an honest and earnest desire to know the truth, particularly in the doctrine of the gospel. It will make the person in reality, what many make high pretences to, without any just ground; i. e. a sincere votary to truth. The main question with him is not, what is esteemed the orthodox doctrine, or what the fashionable divinity? Which is esteemed the most popular, or the most polite? What does Augustine, or Luther, or Calvin, or Arminius say? But the question is, what doth the spirit of Christ, speaking in his word, say? Says the person, amidst so many jarring schemes, and high sanguine pretences, when one says

to here is Christ; and another, so be is there; let me carefully endeavor to find out which is the bible scheme; which is that scheme, that most evidently falls in with the genius of the Christian religion; which is, to hide pride from man; to bumble the vain creature, while it saves him; to empty him of himself; to exalt God; to promote universal holiness. When he has found this, he will adhere to it with an unshaken stability.

2. It will tend to make him a great proficient in the discovery of religious truth. The Israelite indeed, has a mind disposed for the investigation of divine truth. He is got free in some good measure, from his shackles; and so will be apt to make a swifter progress in the knowledge of the truth, that a greater genius which is settled, or sticks fast in the bird lime of prejudice. He seeks knowledge in order to practice; and therefore seeks to have a peculiar claim to this promise, Job. 7. 17. If any man will do his will, he shall know of the doctrine, whether it be of God. He seeks the knowledge of divine truth, not only from books, and conversation, but on his knees, in his closet; hence, he appears directly in the way of that promise, the secret of the Lord is with them that fear him, and he will show them his covenant; (Psal 25. 14, James 1. 5.) or that of the apostle James, in any man lack wisdom, let him ask of God, who giveth literally, to all men, and upbraideth, not, and it shall be given him. The Bible is his favorite book; and hence, it is more likely he shall be able to say, I have more understanding then all my teachers, for thy testimonies are my meditation. (Psal 119. 99.)

3. It will be a good preservation to keep the minister from what is generally understood by trimming. By this I mean, when a minister conceals his own sentiments and this in some of the momentous points in religion; to the end he may keep well with all parties, and offend none. This is a practice as base and cowardly, as it is common. I would charitably hope more to. It is peculiarly unsuitable for a minister of the New Testament, now the veil is taken off from the face of Moses. Such a one use great plainness of speech. (2 Cor. 52. 12.) If the Israelite indeed be a minister, he looks on himself as bound by office to declare the whole counsel

of God; regards himself as a debtor to the wise, and the unwise; and hence, he endeavors to be very circumstantial and explicit; to point out the way of salvation with that plainness, that the wayfaring man, through a fool, should not error therein. In a word, he takes the best pattern for his imitation; I mean the first minister of the sanctuary; who being interrogated concerning his disciples and doctrine, says, I spoke openly to the world; I ever taught in the synagogues, and in the temple, whither the Jews always resort; and in secret I said nothing. (John 18. 29, 20.)

4. It will have a happy tendency to keep a minister from cherishing people's prejudices, and falling in with their favorite humors. This is a practice to which some minister's circumstances lay them under a peculiar temptation; and perhaps I might add, that it is a practice of which some ministers are guilty, who make high pretences to ministerial faithfulness. But let who will be guilty of it, it is not quite right; to say the least of it, it is not strictly honest; it but ill agrees with the character of an Israelite indeed, in whom is no guile.

Such a one would it is true, be very loath to offend one of the least of these little ones, that believe on Christ; but yet he values their souls above their smiles. He would please every man for his good, and to edification, but no further. He endeavors to extirpate their prejudices with a wise indeed, and tender, yet with a faithful hand. He rather chooses to run the risk of displeasing them, than to build them up in any wrong notions of God, or of religion; especially if he looks on the thing to be of a dangerous nature, and what is like to draw after it fatal consequence.

5. It is like to make the minister who is professed of it, a faithful reprover of sin. To reprove and rebuke, is part of the minister's work, as well as to exhort, and perhaps one of the most difficult parts of his work. To do is wisely, seasonably, , humbly, tenderly, and yet faithfully, is no easy thing. But difficult as it is, the minister who is an Israelite indeed, will attempt it. He will cry aloud and not, spare, showing God's people their

transgressions and the house of Jacob their sins. To declaim again sin in general, although with great severity, he does not think sufficient; but he endeavors to be particular, and that he may the better do this, he makes it his business to know what are the prevailing sins of the day, and to show that for these things sake, the wrath of God comes on the children of disobedience. (Eph 4. 6.) Nor does he think it sufficient to be faithful in public reproof; but will use the same in that which is private and personal, if need so require; whatever danger he may incur of the person's hatred and resentment. Although with the Baptist, he have a Herod, a tyrant to deal with, yet he will put his life in his hand, and administer the reproof with an honest plainness.

6. It will make him pay a strict regard to truth, in the characters he gives of men. For instance, if he is to pronounce a funeral eulogium, and in it attempt to give a moral picture of the deceased, he will endeavor that it may be a just one.

If in drawing of a picture, a limner should throw into his piece an undue proportion of the lightsome and glorious colors, and make little or no use of the dark ones; at the same time putting into it every agreeable feature, and concealing the disproportions and defects; would this be painting to the life? Would it be a true picture of the original? I need not wait your answer; the application is easy. If an Israelite indeed, attempts to give a character, he will endeavor that it may suit the person it was intended for. By mentioning what was commendable in the deceased, he willingly gives him his just praise; and although it maybe consistent enough with sincerity, to draw a kind vail over his infirmities, showing them in the shade; yet he will not wholly conceal them; he will be apt to have some such model in his eye as that of Elihu, Job 32. 21, 22. Let me not pray you, accept any man's person, neither let me give flattering titles unto a man. For I know not to give flattering titles, in so doing my maker would soon take me away.

7. The character in my text will powerfully excite the person to endeavor to exhibit to the eyes of spectators, a lovely specimen of

that religion, which he not only professes, but which he preaches to others. Even some of the Heathen insisted upon it as one essential qualification of an orator, that he should be a good man. The faithful minister considers that as all Christians should cause their light to shine before men, so a person in the sacred station, should be exemplary; that his office sets him on an eminence which will render either his vices the more conspicuous. That his preaching Christian virtues and graces, without his practicing them, will be like to have but little effect. For instance, in his preaching to recommend truth to his hearers, while himself is known to be one that will wrong the truth. Or justice, while himself is known to be dishonest. Or humility, while he is evidently lifted up with pride. Or a forgiving spirit, while he indulges an implacable vindictive temper. Hence he endeavors to have a good conversation in all things, that the ministry be not blamed; (2 Cor. 6. 3) in all things, that he may show himself a pattern of good works, so as that he may be able to say, brethren, be ye followers together of me, and mark them that walk so, as ye have us for an example. (Phil 3. 17) Happy minister to whom such a minister, providing they know how to prize and to improve him.

Having spoken to what I proposed in the doctrinal part, I proceed to some practical use of the subject. And among other reflections which it would afford, I take occasion to observe, what my text gives us rule from the mouth of an infallible teacher, by which to judge of characters, and which character we ought to prefer, which is that of a truly honest man, in the sense which has been explained. It is a line much noticed, in a celebrated modern poet, that an honest man is the noblest work of God. (Pope) How mean are the greatest intellectual endowments and human acquirements, if viewed abstractly from the knowledge and the love of God? How poor a figure (says a great modern) must Sir Isaac Newton make, in the eye of the omniscient; (Duncan Forbes Low, President) i. e. on supposition he had only parts and learning, but was destitute of piety? And therefore as the author last quoted adds, these are not the qualifications which claim the Deity's regard. Certainly none will deny that great talents misapplied, is the character of Satan. And if so, then it evidently follows, that the man who having great gifts, prostitutes them to base purposes, does thereby the more nearly resemble the devil.

Let us suppose two characters; one has great parts, to which he has added many considerable acquirements. He is a great linguist, a great mathematician and natural philosopher; he is well versed in history and chronology, ancient and modern, civil and ecclesiastic; he is a good logistician and metaphysician; has a considerable insight into those called the fine arts. His outward deportment is courteous, polite, insinuating. But with all these, and perhaps many more agreeable qualities; he never considers what is due to that being, to whom he owes his all, he saith not where is God my maker? Of the rock that made him, he is unmindful, and forgets God that formed him. (Deut 32. 18.) He is a willing stranger to inward forms of it with great contempt. He hears that man is a fallen creature; and that there is in the bible a most wise and benevolent method for his recovery; but with Gallio, he cares for more of these things. He will not so much as give himself the trouble to dip a little into this divine book; or if he does, it is with a proud, sour, prejudiced mind; so that his natural aversion to the only true religion, is increased. Christ crucified, is to him, as to the ancient Jews and Greeks, a stumbling block and foolishness.

The unhappy fine man, with all his accomplishments, after spending a few years here in an inexcusable neglect of that, which is the beginning of wisdom, is forced to obey the summons of death. His soul appears before him that made it, to receive the just sentence due to those who forgot God. (Psal. 50. 22.)

Let us now take a view of another character. The person it may be has many defects; not so clear a head; not so great a degree of metaphysical acumen as the former; not so much human learning. Perhaps he has not the gift in any eminent degree of ranging his ideas under their proper heads; so that his discourses labor under some sensible degree of obscurity and confusion. He is neither so accurate in his composition, nor so happy in his delivery. He may have more reason then Moses had, to say, O my Lord, I am not eloquent, neither heretofore, nor since thou pakest unto thy servant; but am slow of speech, and of a slow tongue. (Exod. 4. 10) It may be, the person has somewhat of a natural roughness in his temper, which education has not been able effectually to polish; which renders him less agreeable. (This last character of two men, whom a sovereign God was pleased to use as two of the most eminent instruments of promoting religion, I mean, Luther in Germany, and John Knox, by many called the apostle of the Scotto.) But with all these, and many other defects, a gracious God has given the person a serious mind. With humble gratitude he has received the glad tidings of the gospel; and has taken effectual care to avail himself of the great salvation, therein held forth. The native pride of his heart is subdued; the love of God, of Christ, of heaven, has got the better of sin, of self, and of a present world. He is habitually maintaining a warfare against all sin; enduring hardness as a good soldier of Jesus Christ; fighting his way through crowds of external and internal enemies; longing to be perfect, as his father in heaven is perfect. In a word, the person is an Israelite indeed, in the sense of my text, which has been explained. Sirs, put these two characters in contrast in your minds for a moment, and you will soon see which of them ought to be preferred.

Whatever the judgment of the world is, I am satisfied what the judgment of God will be. That the day is approaching, when the righteous will appear to be more excellent than his neighbor. (Prov. 12. 28) And on the other hand, when that which is highly esteemed among men shall appear to be bad in abomination with God. (1 Cor. 4. 15)

Time will not allow me to make several other instances which the subject would naturally lead to; I therefore pass on to a conclusion.

Beloved Brethren, of this Church and congregation,

You have lately been about a piece of heavy work, i. e. laying in the cold and silent grave, the dear remains of one, who had long sustained the office of a spiritual instructor; and who with respect to some of you, I am persuaded could say, though ye had ten thousand instructors in Christ, yet have ye not many fathers, for in Christ Jesus I have begotten you through the gospel. (2 Kings 2. 12.) Daring so long an acquaintance, as above forty years, between a minister and people, who have been mutually happy, it is natural to suppose the affections have struck deep rooting, that consequently the parting is distressing in proportion. I imagine I see a number of you under a considerable degree of the same affection that Elisha was, who although satisfied that his master was gone to heaven, yet under a strong affection from a pungent sense of the great loss which the people of God, and himself in particular had sustained, by the prophet's removal, took hold of his own clothes and rent them to pieces, crying, my father, my father, the chariot of Israel, and the horsemen thereof. (Prov. 31. 2, 8.) Beloved under the present workings of your affections, it is probable you have a strong desire to hear somewhat said to the just praise of the deceased. You think it but right, that the memory of the just should be blessed. And with respect to your late pastor, you have the feelings of the children of the virtuous woman toward their mother, when they rose up and called her blessed. To gratify your just desire, what greater character can I give him who has now left us, than to apply to him who has now left us, than to apply to him, the words of my text, behold an Israelite indeed, in whom is no guile. To a considerable degree of his character, I charitably believe he had a just claim. Should I be more particular and say, that he was an honest, upright man; one that had a just abhorrence of all duplicity and deceit. One who was for going straight forward in that which he took to be duty, leaving events to God. That he not only adhered to true doctrine, but was zealous for it, and appeared to have felt the transforming power of it, on his own heart. That he considered the poor, and devised liberal things. That according to his talent he was a faithful reprover of sin. That he was remarkably temperate with respect to the gratification of animal appetites. That he was a lover of good men; given to hospitality. That he was a good economist. That he appeared to make conscience of family, (and as far as in the nature of the thing could be known) of closet religion. That Joshua's resolution appeared to be his, as for my house we will serve the Lord. That under a variety of domestic trials, his behavior was an honor to the Christian religion. If I should say all these things of him, I doubt not, but many of you could say amen, to each particular; and could from your own personal knowledge, add many other commendable qualities.

I am not afraid to add, and appeal for the truth of it, to those of his intimate acquaintance, who are competent judges, that far from being a mean scholar, he had a very considerable insight into some of the most useful branches of acquired knowledge. I am far from attempting to represent your minister's character while here as represent. Perfection is not the lot of morals in this state of probation. Says a certain author of note, I never knew a perfect clergyman, more than a perfect layman. No Doubt the deceased, while in this state of minority, had his faults; but would it answer any good end? Nay, would it not appear invidious to represent these in their full dimensions and most glaring light, now we hope they are all done away, and he is become one of that glorious company, in whose mouths is found no guile, for they are without fault before the throne of God? (P?? 11. 5.)

Beloved, I do tenderly sympathize with you, the bereaved flock, and family, under our common loss. The deceased was dear to me for many years. We were often jointly engaged in what we esteemed the cause of Christ. We were in journeyings often; exposed to various dangers and fatigues. We frequently joined sweet council, and went up to the house of God in company. But these things are over. He has attained the summit of the heavenly Zion; we are as yet but climbing the hill; and it is likely to have some steep and difficult places to surmount. Let us then press forward with resolution and ardor. Let us be followers of them, who through faith and patience have inherited the promises. (Heb. 6. 12.)

May I not my dear friends, my age, our long acquaintance, and near connections considered, be allowed the freedom of being somewhat particular in a few hints?

Then endeavor to have your spirits thoroughly penetrated with gratitude to the great head of the church, that he was pleased to give you a minister, who obtained mercy of God to be faithful, and to protract his precarious span, until he had arrived at threescore years and ten, the ordinary date of human life.

Ask yourselves as in the presence of the all-knowing God, what improvement you have made under his ministry; and be deeply humbles (if you find there is cause for it) that you have made no better improvement. Labor to recollect as many as possible, of the wholesome and important lessons he often inculcated upon you, with great warmth and with many tears; and by this means diligently endeavor after his decease, to have these things always in remembrance. Thus you will find from happy experience that he being dead yet speaketh.

Think how terrible it would be, if the Godless, Christless, prayerless condition of any of you, should oblige your deceased minister to appear as a witness against you, at the judgment seat. I would add, beware of dejection of spirit, under your present bereavement. You may remember these words, but David encouraged himself in the Lord his God. (Sam. 30. 6.) It was a time of great extremity when David did so. There is always sufficient ground for God's people, to encourage themselves in the Lord their God, let the case be what it will. It is your duty to feel the present stroke, and be deeply affected; to mourn, but not to despond. The servant is dead, but the master is alive. Hear this sweet truth from his own mouth, Rev. 1. 18. I am he that liveth, and was dead; and behold I am alive for evermore. This is not all; Jesus Christ not only lives, but in a state of great opulency, honor and power; so that he has abundant resources richly to supply you, and every bereaved society that put their trust in him. He can make up, yea, more then make up the present breach, great and irreparable as it may seem. Nay, what is more still, he not only can but he will. The tenderness of his bowels infinitely exceeds that of the most affectionate mother towards her sucking child. (Isa. xlix 14, 51) Yea he is not only tender, but infinitely wise. He knows your frame, and remembereth that you are dust. He knows how weak and foolish you are; what dangers you are exposed to, and from what quarter. I would add, see that you love one another. This divine precept is always seasonable, and therefore often inculcated; but is never more seasonable than in your circumstances. You have seen a family of lovely children, when they have newly lost an excellent parent; how all bathed in tears, the dear creatures will fly into each others bosoms, where they mutually pour out their dolorous complaints. Something like it seems to me would be a conduct suitable to your circumstances. Again, be at peace among yourselves. How frequent, how pathetic are the apostolic exhortations, to avoid divisions; to be perfectly joined together; to keep the unity of the spirit in the bond of peace? How pathetically does our dear Lord ask this, in that specimen which he has given us of his intercession work, as one of the best blessings he could ask of his father on the behalf of his people? That they all may be one, as thou father art in me, and I in thee; that they also may be one in us, that the world may believe that thou hast sent me. (John 17. 21.) And if you would keep united, carefully shun the cause of division, of which perhaps pride will be found the principal. Solomon speaks of it as though it were the sole cause, when he says only by pride cometh contention. (Prov. 14. 10.) Let there be no Diotrephes-like spirit among you. Let no man think more highly of himself then he ought to think, but think soberly. It is much more easy to avoid contention when people are at peace, (which is your present happy state) then it is to get out of it, when once they are involved. Hence appears the propriety of the wise man's advise, therefore leave off contention before it be meddled with. (Prov. 17. 14.)

Suffer me to add, don't let the desk be unsupplied, at least let it be so as little as possible. In this I am morally certain, that the Presbytery, to which I am connected, will do what they can that you be agreeably supplied. And while you endeavor to have frequent, or rather constant supplies of preaching, don't be too hasty about a settlement: Make hast slowly, is a wise old proverb. Brethren, the lord has been kind to you; so that instead of being exterminated in your infancy, you have already subsisted as a congregation, upwards of forty years; and from a despicable handful, are become a respectable society. And as it has pleased him, who determines the bounds of his peoples habitations, to situate you in the chief town, of one of the chiefest colonies of British North America; so the honor of God, and religion; the credit of your particular persuasion, and your spiritual education, do all, (under Christ) very much depend on the minister you shall choose. As this then is a matter of weight, act in it with a proportionable caution. Use the wisest and most deliberate steps to secure a happy event. And while you endeavor to act wisely; beware of laying an undue stress on your own wisdom. If you believe that Jesus Christ is the first minister of the sanctuary; that he has the administration of the affairs of the kingdom in his hand; that he is faithful in all his house; that he knows perfectly what qualifications the minister must have, that will suit you; and also, where to find one so qualified, and to send him to you; I say, if you believe these things concerning Christ, (all which you must believe if you are Christians) there can be no more powerful motives to prayer. O then be much in prayer on this important head. Pray to the Lord of the harvest, that he would send forth faithful and suitable laborer into this part of his harvest.

Let me add, have a suitable regard to every surviving branch of the family of your beloved pastor. In particular, let the melancholy and extremely helpless state of his relict, strongly move your compassion for the living, as well as your gratitude to the memory of the dead. Finally,

To the child of the deceased here present, I would say, if you are the child of God, (as charity bids me believe) however, the world may forget you soon, yet Christ remainest yours with an unchangeable and most tender affection. The world is changeable; but he is not immutable. Jesus Christ is the same yesterday, today, and forever. He is the very same compassionate savior, as when he groaned in spirit, and wept at the grave of Lazarus. In all your afflictions, he is afflicted; he puts tears in his bottle. If then you put your trust in him, and have recourse to him in your distress, you will find him to be the friend who sticketh closer than a father, than a brother, than all earthly relations. Let me add, in the midst, of your mourning be thankful to God that he gave you such a parent; that he continued him with you so long; that he was not snatched away from your tender infancy; but that you had the benefit of a genteel, and what was more, a religious education, under his paternal eye. Let this encourage you to put your trust in God. Ungrateful and giddy as the world is, you can hardly lack friends among so many of your father's old acquaintance and friends. But be that as it will, by all means endeavor to ensure the covenant favor of him, who loves his own to the end. Who always makes good the promise, I will never leave thee, nor forsake thee.

THE VOICE of the PROPHETS CONSIDERED IN A DISCOURSE or SERMON,

Showing what is Wisdom for men in a Fallen Estate;

And also, what is Wisdom for a People in a Civil State.

With an Observation on This Time.

But where shall wisdom be found, and where is the place of understanding.   Job.

Should ye not bear the words which the Lord hath cried by the former prophets, when Jerusalem was inhabited and in prosperity? Zechariah.

Printed in the Year M,DCC,LXXVI. (1776)
This is Rev. McGregor's last recorded sermon, he died the following year on May 3, 1777

Prov. 9. 12.

If thou be wise, thou shall be wise for the self; but if thou scornest, thou alone shall bear it.

et us consider that we are in the presence of an Holy God, who made us, and gives us every good thing we enjoy; who will bring every work into judgment with every secret thing. It becomes us therefore with the utmost awe and reverence, to behave ourselves so as not to break his holy law, or merit his divine displeasure. You may remember, that within these few years past there has been several judgments threatened against this land and nation. The first that I shall mention was in what is commonly called the Chebucto fleet, a large fleet sent from France against the colonies; big enough according to humane understanding, to have destroyed our shipping, and at least to have laid our sea ports in the utmost ruin and desolation. The English fleet at that time by contrary winds, a mere act of providence, hindered from coming to our relief. But mark, the French fleet taken with a dreadful distemper on their passage; they put into Chebucto, where they died by the thousands, and were not suffered to do the colonies the least damage.

A Case something similar to what we have told us, Judg. 7. 2. And the Lord said unto Gideon, the people that are with thee are too many for me to give the Midianites into their hands; lest Israel want themselves against me, saying, mine own hands hath saved me.

Another instance of judgment threatened against us, was in the beginning of the last war, General Braddick was defeated by French and Indians, who came in like a flood on some of the southern colonies, burning houses, killing and taking captive many of our people; it seemed as though they devour the whole land. But mark in the conclusion of the war, the French quite from St. Lawrence River to the Mississippi, were brought into subjection. Which brings to my mind the prophecy of Amos, who after he had reproved Israel for divers fins, says, chap. 7. 1. Thus hath the Lord showed unto me, and behold he formed grasshoppers in the beginning of the shooting up of the latter growth, and so, it was the latter growth, after the king's mowings. And it came to pass, that when they had made an end of eating the grass of the land, then I said, O lord, forgive, I beseech thee; by whom shall Jacob arise? For he is small. The Lord repented for this. It shall not be, saith the Lord. Thus hath the Lord God showed unto me, and behold, the Lord had called to contend by fire, and it devoured the great deep, and did eat up a part. Then said I, O Lord God, cease, I beseech thee; by whom shall Jacob arise? For he is small. The Lord repented for this. This also shall not be, faith the Lord God. Then said the Lord, behold, I will set a plum-line in the midst of my people Israel. Have we not reason to believe, from these signs, that there is something among us that is very offensive in the eyes of a holy God that must be reformed, ere we can expect to prosper. O that the Lord would spare his people! It maybe that they will repent. Are we now engaged in a more dreadful war, blood a running, killing one another? As in Rev. 6 .4.

I do not determine wherefore it is that the hand of the Lord is gone out against us. I shall only observe, that God sometimes brings his judgments by instruments, to whom his people have done no wrong; see Judges 10. 6, and onward, and the children of Israel did evil again in the sight of the Lord, and served Baalim and Ashtareth. And the anger of the Lord was hot against Israel, and he sold them into the hands of Philistines, and into the hands of the children of Ammon. And what harm had the children of

Judah done to the Babylonians? Yet how they destroyed and captivated them! But what was the matter? See Jer. 7. 5 – 7. If ye thoroughly amend your ways, and your doings; if ye thoroughly execute judgment between a man and his neighbor; if ye oppress not the stranger, the fatherless, and the widow, and shed not innocent blood in this place, neither walk after other gods, to your hurt; then will I cause you to dwell in this place, in the land that I gave your fathers, forever and ever.

But it is possible some of you may say, at least in your hearts, "We are wise men, and understand our interest exceeding well; who can teach us? But I desire you to remember, that even the wisest of men have sometimes need of being , and in mind of things they well knew. I will therefore consider the words in the following order,

First, endeavor to show from the scripture, what is true wisdom for men in a fallen condition.

And in the next place, endeavor to show what is true wisdom for a people in a civil state.

Thirdly, that whosoever shall scorn the word of God, that they alone shall bear it.

And lastly, Show, in some measure, what it is they shall bear.

First, what is wisdom for men in a fallen state? But let us first observe, that there is what hath been called wisdom, see Daniel 5. 15. And now the wise men, the Astrologers; who were probably such men, as by the help of the devil, pretended to foretell future events; but this is so far from the true wisdom intended in the text, that it is the most dreadful folly.

Another sort of wisdom is mentioned in Cor. 2. 13. Which things also we speak not in the words which mans wisdom teacheth, but which is called man's wisdom; of this sort of wisdom, I suppose the apostle Paul had a large share before his conversion, being brought up to learning, who had the witness of miracles, and zealous in what he called religion; yet persecuted the Christians until he received a light from heaven.

We have an account, John 3. of Nichodemus likewise a ruler of the Jews, who probably had a great share of human understanding or man's wisdom, although he was so far convinced by the miracles, that he said to our Savior, Rabbi, we know that thou art a teacher come from God, for no man can do these miracles that thou dost, except God be with him. Yet when our Savior told him, except a man be born again, he cannot see the kingdom of God, he understands nothing of this by his human wisdom, but says, how can a man be born when he is old? And further faith, how can these things be? How ignorant was he of the new birth, or the new heart which delighteth in hallelujahs and adoration to God! And we are told in plain words, Cor. 2. 14. But the natural man receiveth not the things of the spirit of God, for they are foolishness unto him; neither can he know them, because they are spiritually discerned. And our Savior himself says, John 6. 45. It is written in the prophets, and they shall be all taught of God. Every man therefore that hath heard and learned of the father, cometh unto me.

My answer then to the first question (which is, what is wisdom for men in a fallen estate?) shall be, that it is their wisdom to go to God by solemn prayer, for his mercy in teaching them, and to bring them into true religion by his mighty power, and that with an honest intention to be conformed to the will of God; for God is a spirit and in truth, John 4. 24. For if the heart doth not believe that God is righteous to reject its request, the prayer is like a demand; and it is therefore the wisdom of sinners to beg of God to show them how vile they are, and know that God is sovereign of his gifts, or they would cease to be free grace. And I hope there are none of you so wise in your own eyes, as to think you have no need that God should teach you. Have you more wit than Nichodemus, or St. Paul, who were both taught of God? And indeed, could men go to the heaven by their won wit and invention, to whom would they sing praise? Would it be to themselves, while they neglect or despise to glorify God? What, self-saved, and self-glorified! No; if any are saved, it must be by the gift of God.

Which brings me to the second place, to say, that whosoever shall scorn to beg of God, to renew his heart, and so be taught, he alone shall bear it; for it is written, 'As I live, saith the Lord, every knee shall bow to me, and every tongue shall confess to God. So then every one of us shall give an account of himself to God,' Rom. 14. 11, 12. 'Be not deceived, God is not mocked, for whatsoever a man soweth, that shall he also reap; for he that soweth to his flesh, shall of the flesh reap corruption; but he that soweth to the spirit, shall of the spirit reap life everlasting,' Gal. 6. 7, 8. And the text is a full confirmation of this. 'If thou scorneth, thou alone shalt hear it.' But what shalt he bear; the answer is, 'The Lord Jesus shall be revealed from heaven with his mighty angels in flaming fire, taking vengeance on them that know not God, and that obey not the gospel of our Lord Jesus Christ; who shall be punished with the everlasting destruction from the presence of the Lord, and from the glory of his power,' 2. Thesl. 1. 7, 8, 9. 'Then shall he say also unto them on the left hand, depart from me ye cursed, into everlasting fire, prepared for the devil and his angels,' Mat. 25. 41. The son of man shall send forth his angels, and they shall gather out of his kingdom all things that offend, and them that do iniquity, and shall cast them into a furnace of fire, there shall be wailing and gnashing of teeth,' Mat. 13. 41, 42. 'And I say unto you my friends, be not afraid of them that kill the body, and after that have no more that they can do. But I will forewarn you, whom you shall fear, fear him which after he hath killed the body, hath power to cast into hell. Yea, I say unto you, fear him,' Luke, 12. 4. Can any person get any thing by scorning or fighting the counsels of their maker; to be cast into everlasting fire, prepared for the devil and his angels, where the soul dies not, and the fire is not quenched. I conclude this point, with this word; fly from the wrath to come.

In the next place, or secondly, I shall endeavor to show what is wisdom for men in a civil state. To this I answer, it is wisdom for a people to do righteously, or what is the same, to keep the ten commands, for we have the words of the most high and holy God, the former of al things, see Deut. 16. 20. 'That which is altogether just shalt thou follow, that thou mayest live and inherit the land which the lord thy God giveth thee.' Levit. 18. 5. 'Ye shall therefore keep my statutes, and my judgments, which if a man do, he shall live in them: I am the Lord.'

For instance; suppose a people should have no law to punish the breaking any one of the four of these commands, and of consequence have no regard to God; ho dreadful must be their doom: see what was said to the children of Israel; go and cry unto the gods which ye have chosen, let them deliver you in the time of tribulation, Judges, 10. 14.

Let us under the fifth command, which is, honor thy father and mother, that thy days may be long upon the land which the Lord thy God giveth thee. Now if there were no obedience or respect paid to parents, or others, how would every villain invade the property of others, spending their time in it so that there could be no sustenance for people; and if there were no law against murder, how would people be in danger of losing their lives, it would doubtless take so much time in preserving them, as that they would not be able to raise any support for life.

And see what is said against breaking the seventh command. Jeb. 31. 11. 'For this is a heinous crime, yea, it is an iniquity to be punished by the judges, for it is a fire that consumed to destruction, and would root out all mine increase. And with respect to the eighth command, were there no law to punish stealing, how would many think it easier to steal for a living, than to labor, which of natural consequence, will ruin any people, and witness is the eyes of the law; how could the breaking of any one of these commands be punished, if there were nothing but false witness; and the tenth command, which includes the whole, or any honesty to our neighbor, to be neglected will be equally ruinous.

But you will doubtlessly ask in a more particular manner, when a nation, or a people, may be truly said to break any one of these commands? To this I answer, that a people, or nation, may be guilty of one villain's stealing a horse, for when the judges willingly and knowingly, clear the thief, when they know he is guilty, they are partakers with the thief; and indeed, for what of a proper enquiry into truth, they may become guilty. So when a people shall see their judges do unrighteousness, and willingly clear the thief; if they do not endeavor to know and displace such judges, they all become guilty; for the people are commanded to see that righteousness takes place: see Deut. 16. 18. Judges and officers shalt thou make thee in all thy gates, which the Lord thy God giveth thee, throughout thy tribes; and they shall judge the people with just judgment.

This command was given to the people, they out therefore to have put in officers by election, and to be sure to be left out when they did not do righteously. What greater encouragement to the wicked, than hinder their being found out and punished; how severely were the children of Israel punished when they made no judges, but left every man to do as he pleases, or that which was right in his own eyes; see the end of judges: should they not have made righteous judges a terror to evil doers, how guilty then of the blood of the Levites wife, and how dangerous was it to put in officers for life, if the people were justly charged for what they knew, and suffered their representatives to do.

Again kings or rulers may be greatly to blame another way. For instance, suppose a king, or rulers, should take from the people, ninety nine parts of an hundred of the produce from the people, or the value, and lay it up for themselves, or give it to petitioners, or charity men, and enable them to carry on rioting, and drunkenness, while the people are greatly distressed to maintain it; it may be as great a burden, as to be slaves: and how wicked is it to rate the people to maintain rioting, and drunkenness, right in the face of God's commands, for even kings are not to make themselves rich beyond bounds with the peoples money, see Deut. 17. 17. Neither shall be greatly multiply to himself silver and gold. Nevertheless, there is no doubt but that kings and rulers ought to have a reasonable and honorable recompense for their labor, See Rom. 13. 6. For this cause pay you tribute also for they are God's ministers, attending continually upon this very thing.

I should think it proper, under this enquiry, for us to consider the construct of the children of Israel, and see wherein they were blamed, and when they were not. For God is the same, yesterday, today, and forever? Therefore those things that were displeasing to him than, are displeasing to him now if they are acted. And I do not remember any threatening against the children of Israel for injustice, until after Solomon's time: the question will then be, how did they construct in that time? See Deut. 24. 10. When thou dost lend thy brother anything thou shalt not go unto his house to fetch his pledge. Did they indeed when they fold, or lent one another anything, take a pledge as a witness to the debt? I answer, doubtless they did; or what is the meaning of a pledge. Wherefore it is evident they took care beforehand to know how to do justice. But see Deut. 24. 12, 13. And if the man be poor, thou shalt not sleep with his pledge. In any case thou shalt deliver him the pledge again when the sun goeth down.

Why truly did they not trust one another longer than from morning to night; for what profit could a pledge be that must be given up before the dept was paid. I answer, that the creator could show the pledge to a number of the neighbors, and thereby get witnesses that the debtor owes for goods delivered? In that case a creditor might recover his cause, or else it was lost, for what advantage was it to have a pledge or witnesses, if a person could recover upon his own say-so, or by making a false book, and swear it was truly and justly charged, nor could they make a book against any person for four times so much as the debtor would have given a pledge for; nor for things for which satisfaction had been made. Should they not have been as really punished had they had no law to prevent making false accounts, as they were for not having law, or judges, to prevent the wickedness done to the

Levites wife; wherefore they did well to take care beforehand, that one should not defraud or wrong another. If we can find their practice, what was the mind and will of God, let us hear it. But to return; it is probable, when persons through themselves wronged, and could get no pledge; they went immediately to trial. I shall here produce the account of an action that was brought and tried in one of their courts, present, King Solomon judge, 1. Kings, 3. 16, to the end. They came there two women that were harlots, unto the king, and stood before him: and the one woman said, O my Lord, I, and this woman dwell in one house; and I was delivered a child with her in the house: and it came to pass, the third day after that I was delivered, that this woman was delivered also, and we were together: there was no stranger with us in the house; save we two in the house. And this woman's child died in the night, because she overlaid it. And she arose at midnight and took my son from beside me, while thine hand maid slept, and laid it in her bosom, and laid her dead child in my bosom; and when I rose in the morning to give my child suck, behold it was dead; but when I had considered it in the morning, behold it was not my son which I did bear: and the other woman said ney; but the living is my son, and the dead is thy son: and this said no, but the dead is thy son, and the living is my son. Thus they spoke before the king. Then said the king, the one saith this is my son liveth, and thy son is the dead: and the other saith nay; but thy son is the dead, and my son is the living. And the king said bring me a sword, and they brought a sword before the king; and the king said divide the living child in two, and give half to the one, and half to the other. Then spoke the woman who's the living child was, unto the king (for her bowels yearned upon her son) and she said, O my lord, give her the living child, and in no wise slay it: But the other said, let it be neither mine, nor thine, but divide it. Then the king answered and said, give her the living child, and in no wise slay it; she is the mother thereof. And all Israel heard of the judgment which the king had judged, and they feared the king; for they saw that the wisdom of God was in him to do judgment.

Here observe we have no account of any writ, or any officer to bring the defendant before the king, for it likely was looked upon as a token of guilt, to be unwilling to attend the court: we have no account of any attorney to abate the writ, or plead demurer, or special plea; nor even to say, that the plaintiff had produced no witness to prove her cause; neither could they go from court, to court, until they had spent in the trial, three times so much as the cause was worth. But the judge hears the story from the parties, and by policy finds out from them which was the true mother, and orders, that she should have her own child.

But where lay the great wisdom think you; was it in judging that a woman should have her own child, or in searching the matter.

See what is spoken by Job, who seems to have been a judge: chap. 29. 16. I was a father to the poor, and the cause which I knew not, I searched out. I break the jaws of the wicked, and plunk the spoil out of his teeth.

But from Solomon's time, to their going into captivity, there are repeated threatenings for injustice, and violence, see Micah. 2. 1. Woe to them that devise iniquity, and work evil upon their beds: when the morning is light, they practice it because it is power of their hands. And they covet fields, and take them by violence, and houses, and take them away: So they oppress a man and his house, even a man and his heritage. Therefore, thus saith the Lord; behold against this family do I devise an evil, from which ye shall not remove your necks: see also Jer. 22. 3. Thus saith the Lord; execute ye judgment, and righteousness; and deliver the spoiled out of the hands of the oppressor; and do no wrong; do no violence to the stranger, the fatherless, nor the widow; neither shed innocent blood in this place; for if you do this thing, indeed then shall there enter in the gates of this house, kings setting upon the throne of David riding in chariots, and on horses, he and his servants, and his people. But if ye will not hear these words, I swear by myself, saith the Lord; that this house shall become a desolation.

But they do all this injustice, and violence, without any pretence of law? No, they did not; for we read, Micah. 6. 16. For statutes of Omry are kept, and all the works of the house of Ahab; and Hab. 1. 4. Therefore the law is stacked, and judgment doth never go forth, for the wicked doth compass about the righteous; therefore wrong judgment proceedeth.

But what was their law do you think; was it like a fishnet, that would catch all the little fish, and let all the great fish go through? I answer yes; it probably was: but you will ask, wow can that be? I answer, that under a plausible pretence of doing justice; that when either partly thought themselves wronged, they might review or appeal, from court, to court; until they had spent three times so much in the trial, as the cause was worth. The great men, by having very large fees for managing the causes, probably run off with the most of the money, while they left the poor to suffer for want. Who having recovered hardly enough to pay the cost, they lost all that was taken from them by injustice, or violence. How did this deliver the spoiled? And when any one person did injustice, or violence to another, he was obliged to go to law, or loose his right; and who knows but what that was next to his life; was not this nation guilty of this. And what were they better to have a law which cost more than could be recovered by it; could it relieve a distressed person who had been wronged by injustice or violence. But if the righteous lost all, what became of the mistaken party, who likely lost more than three times all. Was not such a law, like an iron brier, that tore the flesh off everyone that came near it: wherefore every mite of cost that was made in trails more than was absolutely necessary, was unjust; no better than injustice. Let us conclude this point, with these words, 2 Chro. 19. 6. To the judges, take heed what ye do, for ye judge not for man, but for the Lord, who is with you in judgment. And whosoever shall break any one of the laws of God, they alone shall bear it: for if a people shall have no law to punish the breaking any of these commandments, this is the natural tendency to bring them to ruin, as has been observed before; if a people shall carefully punish the breakers of these commands, it is strange if anyone escapes without punishment, shame, and disgrace; however, they will certainly be under the curse, see Deut. 27. 6. Cursed be that confirmeth not all the words of this text reach them; and all the people shall say amen. Observe the word confirm; for all are required to confirm this law. Therefore, here is a curse pronounced against everyone who has a right to choose rulers who doth not endeavor to choose such as will be most likely to keep this law.

Here is a curse pronounced against everyone who doth endeavor to know what rulers do not do well in keeping this law; who shall throw away his power, or doth not endeavor to displace, or leave out such rulers as do not do well in keeping this law. Here is a curse pronounced against everyone who although he has not a right to choose rulers eye or ear who shall do anything which he knows is likely to hinder the keeping this law. Here is a curse pronounced against every judge or other who shall not endeavor the keeping this law. In fine, here is a curse pronounced against all the breakers of this law: and who hath ever hardened himself against his creator, and hath prospered; therefore, everyone that scorneth he alone shall bear it. But what shall he hear? I answer, that whosoever shall scorn to obey the law of God, shall bear his wrath and displeasure. See what (if it be practiced) will be an instance of this, Exed. 22. 22. Ye shall not afflict any widow, or fatherless child; if thou afflict them in any wise, and they cry at all unto me, I will surely bear their cry; and my wrath shall wax hot. And I will kill you with the sword; and your wives shall be widows, and your children fatherless. And I have heard there is a distemper among the nations, which is the most dreadful and mortal to the well people, for when a number of men shall make unjust rules they will not only enjoy the displeasures of God, but they, and their's must be tried by the law, see Prev. 38. 10. Whoso causeth the righteous to go astray in evil way, shall fall himself into his own pit; but the upright shall have good things in possession: and Job. 18. 8. For he is cast into dust by his own feet, and he walketh upon a snare. I remember an old observation of (missing text p 15) maid. That when the children of Israel had (missing text p 15), to whom they heard so much as that they could excuse the laws, they always prospered on the other hand, when they had bad rulers, to whom they heard, they suffered greatly: and those rulers fared the worst, witness Jereboam, Jehoiachim Baasha, and Ahab. I conclude this point with that in Job. 27. 8. For what is the hope of a hypocrite, though he hath gained, when God taketh away his soul.

And now let us conclude this part with a word of exhortation to the hearers. As we are probationers here, for eternity: Let us set apart some time in every day, wherein to consider solemnly what will become of us in another world; and if we are in any distress, and see that the rod of God is upon us; let us mistrust whether there be not something in our practice that we have overlooked, that is offensive to any holy God. Let us seek to God by fasting and prayer, to teach us what is amiss. See the example of David, when there was three years famine, year after year. And David enquired of the Lord, 2. Samuel, 21. 1. Let us examine carefully how our actions agree with the rules of the word of God, see Zach. 7. 7. Should ye not hear the words which the Lord hath cried by the former prophets: and whatever is amiss let us reform, and restore righteousness, then by fasting and prayer seek to God for Forgiveness, and mercy; who can tell if God will direct, and prosper our enterprise, or find a way of redemption, that we perish not. I conclude the whole, with that in Isa. 50. 10. Who is among you that fearest the Lord; that walketh in darkness, and hath no light: Let him trust in the name of the Lord, and stay upon his God.

AMEN

Credits and sources.

Willey's Book of Nutfield - George Franklin Willey 1895.

New Hampshire Historical Society

Derry Museum of History & Richard Holmes

University of New Hampshire at Durham

United States Library of Congress

Chester Historical Society (Vermont)

Immigrants in the Land of Canaan – Miller, Schrier, Boling, Doyle

Appendix
About William M. Gorman

A 6th Great Grandson of Rev. David McGregor, through his daughter Margret McGregor who married Colonel James Rogers of the famous Rogers' Rangers and King's Rangers, born 1726, his son James Rogers born 1764, his son David Rogers born 1805, his daughter Mary Allen Rogers born 1845, her son Robert D. Gorman born 1876, his son Leland W. Gorman born 1906 and his son Robert W. Gorman born 1932. All of them are gone now and all were very proud to be related to the famous James and Robert Rogers of Rogers' Rangers.

I got involved in researching my family's history to complete the research started by my late mother, Arlene, who in 1972, took my siblings and I on a cross country trip looking up records and searching graveyards for ancestors. Since then I have made a tremendous addition to her efforts. Sadly her ancestors have been very difficult to trace. We visited Sandhurst, Ontario where a Historical marker for Colonel James Rogers stands. I believe the marker, the church and grave yard are on lot 7 where James lived and his grave is here but missing the head stone. The Rogers side of the family is on my father's side, he is also descended from the Hopkins of the Mayflower and the Jones family that arrived with Captain Smith in Virginia. Aside from my native American ancestors, next year will be the 400th anniversary of my ancestors immigration to America. Nearly a dozen of my ancestors fought in the American Revolution and a few in the Civil War including my great great grandfather, Christopher Darius Gorman. He served in the Wisconsin 8th Infantry with Old Abe the Screaming War Eagle.

I previously published a 2007 edition of Robert Rogers' "A Concise Account of North America, originally written in 1765, In which on page 12 my 10th Great Grandfather Major General Robert Sedgwick is mentioned, he took Port Royal in 1654. Rev. David McGregor's son, Robert built the first bridge over the Merrimack River and daughter Mary is the grandmother of Jane Means Appleton, wife of President Franklin Pierce. Other famous ancestors include Captain James Avery of Groton, Connecticut of which Avery point is named for. Samuel L. Clemmons is a 3rd cousin. My family's linage includes over 100 King, 100 Queens and hundreds of princes and princesses of every Kingdom in Europe. Lady Godiva is also an ancestor, turns out she was likely in her 60's or 70's when she made her ride, she was born about 980 and the ride was in the second half of the eleventh century.

My 4thGreat Grandfather, James Rogers III married Mary Allen born in 1775, who may be the daughter of Ethan Allen. I believe after Ethan's death her step-mother, Fanny, in her greed wrote her off as dead for marring a loyalist who owned close to 50,000 acres. Fanny did this to prevent Mary from inheriting any of her father's lands. James Rogers III but several of his relatives through collage with money from land sales. His brother David McGregor Rogers was a prominent member of Canada's Parliament.

I am currently living in Klamath Falls, Oregon and working on a 3rd book and some movie scripts. I also maintain the Descendants of James Rogers web site at Montalona.com and work on family related research projects.

www.ingramcontent.com/pod-product-compliance
Lightning Source LLC
Chambersburg PA
CBHW071622170426
43195CB00038B/1777